AYE BELONG TO GLASGOW

JIMMY DOC

AYE BELONG TO GLASGOW

iUniverse books may be ordered through booksellers or by contacting:

iUniverse
1663 Liberty Drive
Bloomington, IN 47403
www.iuniverse.com
844-349-9409

ISBN: 978-1-6632-4788-9 (sc)
ISBN: 978-1-6632-4787-2 (e)

Print information available on the last page.

iUniverse rev. date: 11/16/2022

FOREWORD

To say Jimmy Doc that is one of a kind personality would be an understatement.

In twenty years of ghostwriting, I have never met anyone quite like him.

How did our work together start?

Our relationship started with a phone call out of the blue. It was a summer afternoon and I was driving to a cafe where I was going to work the rest of the day. I was turning off the highway when a call came through on my iPhone. A large number of prospective customers call me straight off my website, so I'm accustomed to picking up strange numbers, usually disappointed when it's someone calling to extend my vehicle's warranty or help with the student loans I've long since paid off.

This wasn't one of those calls though. It was Jimmy Doc and he had a wild hair about getting this book out there in the world.

"Just tell me if it's shite, Erick, and I'll move on not bother you again."

No delusions of grandeur, I like that.

I won't steal Jimmy's thunder by giving away the sock in the gut you'll get by turning the page and reading his first chapter. I will say, however, that diving into his unedited manuscript was an experi- ence I won't soon forget. I got a good laugh. Then it made me think. Then I kept on reading.

It's a good day when the books I work on are as entertaining as the ones I read for pleasure.

This is one of those rare pleasurable, enter- taining reads. I think you will agree.

— Erick Mertz

1

A STAR IS BORN

I had a real, honest to God, afro when I was born. See the picture if you don't believe me.

By all accounts my mother and father started sleeping together around September/October 1951. A wee bit out of step for the time, don't you think? How do I know this? Because my mother told me. She didn't mean to. She just got flummoxed one morning while distracted.

We were in the kitchen, and she was cooking breakfast. I was reading my comics. "Mom?"

"Yes, dear?"

"Was I born prematurely?" I swallowed. Curious as to the answer.

"No," she said, "Why?"

"Because," I explained, "you got married in November 1951 and I was born on the 4th of June

1952." My mother and I never had conversations like this. Anything barely controversial, in a Scottish household at the time, was avoided like disease. Especially sex. I was watching her closely, enjoying her discomfort. Just a little. It was fun tugging on Superman's cape for once. If my dad would've been there, I'd have gotten clipped round the ear.

Years later my granny Doc told me they both came to her and confessed they'd been bang at it for months and the inevitable happened. I'm assuming the actual conversation was a wee bit sweeter, more delicate than that, but I don't know. Like many things in my life, I really don't know Why, How, When or even Who....... or What the hell.

Anyway, I came into this world in a hospital in Glasgow called Rotten Row. I was the firstborn. Even- tually, I ended up with three sisters and two brothers. The name Rotten Row was derived from a road in medieval times, ROUTE DE ROI. Kings Road. Who knew? When I was born I was 8 pounds 1 ounce.

Strange thing, I remember seeing a list of my brothers' and sisters' birth weights and remember thinking they're all in order. Me... 8 pounds 1 ounce. Linda... 8 pounds 2 ounces. Jane... 8 pounds

3 ounces and so on. 1 potato, 2 potato, 3 potato 4. What a regi- mented bunch of ne'er do wells. How many times did they do well?...NE'ER. Not really. That's not true.

In fact, they all did pretty well. Linda got married and became a successful hairdresser with her own store. Jane was married and became quite a sought- after public speaker. Elaine married, had four kids and could play a multitude of musical instruments. Alan, I don't really know but he seems to be happy with life.

I know my youngest brother, Garry. He's the only one I really know. I don't know the others and they don't know me. I left home too early and was of a different generation. One of the reasons I'm writing this.

By all accounts, I was a healthy baby but spoiled absolutely rotten. I blame the hospital for that. Really? Rotten Row?

Not really. Though I know why I was a spoiled little douchebag. Because I was surrounded all alone by adoring women for three years. And because my father was in the army.

My granny Docherty loved me and showed it. So did my granny Findlay but she was shy and had been treated so badly by her father who kicked her out of the house when she was 14 because his new wife hated her. So she was reluctant to show her feelings. At least that's how I saw it. Always felt sorry for my granny Findlay. She lost the love of her life, her husband, to cancer when he was 57 years old. I think this soured her to life a little. My grandfather would sit me on his knee, tear off small pieces of paper, lick them and stick them on his nose and breathe "Pigeons" making the papers fly. At three years old I thought this was hilarious.

I stayed with my granny Findlay when I returned from Iceland. We would sit by the fire in her living room lit only by gaslight, and she would tell me how she missed touching his skin at night when they slept together. My granny was truly in love but in a different, less carnal way than I think my parents shared.

My granny Docherty would share jokes with me. I'll never forget sitting across from her at the Sunday dinner table when I was about 11. It was a living room that became a dining room on Sundays. The adults and I sat at the big table. I was allowed to sit with the grownups because I was nearly six feet tall and would've looked stupid at the kids' table. That was my thought anyway.

The Sunday meal was roast beef with gravy, roast potatoes and peas. To this day the tastiest meal I've ever had. Every Sunday it was the same.

I never tired of it. To this day it's still my favorite meal. Working class until I die, I guess.

My grandfather was at the head of the table next to me, kinda grumpy as usual, and I was opposite my granny. At the other end of the table was my father, the oldest son. Deep in thought, thinking about money and how to make it. Next to him was my uncle Davy, a railway worker who my father said had loose screws in his head brought about by his job and wife. My father reasoned the time schedules he was forced to keep by British rail and his wife had robbed him of the wee bit o' sense he had. Opposite him was my uncle Stevie with his wife. Stevie was just married and pussy whipped, so nobody paid him much attention.

Around this time my granddad was at the begin- ning of Alzheimer's disease. He was a man of maybe five feet nine inches, stocky with a big nose, full head of white hair and hands like an 8-day clock. Big, gnarly, calloused hands. A working man's hands.

He had been a pick and shovel man who worked his way up to foreman over his career. He was retired now but at the time of his retirement, he had been in charge of 500 men with picks and shovels who obeyed him or were fired.

He worked for the Scottish Electricity Board laying and spanning cable all across Scotland. He had been retired now for eight years and his dementia was beginning to be obvious.

There was a low murmur at the table and my granddad leans over to my granny and says, "Who's that big guy at the other end of the table?"

My granny says, patting my grandad's hand, "Steve, you know who that is. That's your oldest son, Jimmy."

A few minutes pass and my granddad leans over again and says, "Who's that other guy?"

My granny says, "That's your middle son, Davy." Again, a pause for thought.

He leans over again.

"Who's that other big guy?" His sons were all six feet tall.

My granny says, "That's your other son, Stevie." He thinks about this for a while then blurts out, "HOW MANY FUCKIN' SONS DO I HAVE?"

My granny and I nearly wet ourselves. My granny had an adventurous spirit and a wicked sense of humor which she showed years later in flying from Scotland to Hawaii to see me when she was 96 years old. A ballsy old broad. Halfway round the world at 96. Makes me tired just thinking about it.

Here I must mention British Airways. I sent my granny $1000 saying it was for a ticket to come visit me. I never thought she'd do it. I didn't think it was enough for a start, and traveling that distance at that age... No chance. I thought she'd just keep the money and spend it on her grandkids. Not only did she get a ticket, and traveled to Hawaii from Glasgow, they flew her first class. Astounding. A different era.

A few seconds go past and when the initial shock leaves, everybody is rolling around pissing them- selves, laughing. That was a good day. Cemented the bond between my granny and me and unfortunately, displayed the rift between my father and me. It's the only time I recall laughing *with* my father. Sad.

My aunts loved me too, as well as both my grand- mothers. Meanwhile, I was left in this totally female world, totally bereft of male company. It wasn't his choice. He was conscripted. At that time, every able- bodied man and some able-bodied women were forced to do military service. After World War Two just about everybody in Europe had to serve in some fashion. I was born in 1952 and this would be around 1956.

I don't think this would be a problem for most people but, for me, because I was getting my ass kissed left and right, nook to cranny, for years. It was an absolute stab in the neck with a sharp instrument when my father returned. I wasn't pleased. To say the least. I don't recall much about the day I actually met my father. I was three. But given the memories I do have, I'll bet it was not a happy day.

My granny Doc told me I hated my father as soon as I met him. My granny told me I kicked and fussed and was in general a little shit. Probably because he had the audacity to tell me "No" – maybe the first dose of discipline I'd ever encountered. He was just out of the army after three years and probably forgot how civilian life worked. Apart from the fact he really was a bit of an ass. I don't mean this in a milquetoast namby-pamby way. He was a tough guy. I've seen him fight.

He would get angry. Violently angry. He would beat me. Hard. Not when I was three. Seven, eight and nine was a different story. He wasn't an ogre. He was a sergeant in the army and was probably used to being obeyed.

A couple of times my mother had to tell him to stop. "That's enough, Jimmy." I wonder did she ever realize that she was the bitch that caused it all?

She was not an ill-intentioned girl, my mother, but like most of my relatives and acquaintances, she was unsophisticated and trying to claw her way out of poverty. Perception was extremely important to my mammy.

My mother, when shopping for underwear, never shopped at the "Lingerie" department. She shopped at the "ling ger eh" department. Not the "lawn zzher ray" department. She knew how the word was spelled, just had never heard it pronounced.

Like my granny Findlay, her mother, who, her whole life was convinced the Orangutan was pronounced the "Orange u tang."

This is neither good nor bad, just an observation. Shit, I sound so fucking pompous. Anyway, between social pressures to advance and pinching every penny to survive and having, eventually, six kids, it's no wonder she was overwhelmed and had a bad 'tude.

My father would come home from work, I kind of assume in a happy mood. He was an auto mechanic who was well respected at work. He was foreman in the "Corporation." This was a city job. That in itself was prestigious. He was the guy who kept the double-decker buses running. Nobody had a car back then. Mid 50s. But we did.

She would greet him at the door, not with a kiss and a smile but with a list of complaints about what we had done that day to fucking piss her off. It wasn't just me. There were five of us at the time of this recollection. Garry wasn't born yet. My sisters were subjected to the same abuse as I, but not as violent. They were girls so therefore treated differently. Maybe they were not as terrified as I was. Maybe they saw a limit to his violence. I did not.

He hit me one time while he was drinking a cup of tea. Apparently, I had done something to cheese him or my mother off. I don't remember exactly what it was. He was standing by the fire. I was sitting on the sofa. He strode forward about to give me the back of his hand. He forgot (I hope) he was holding a mug in his hand and swiped at me. I, in return, put up my forearm to fend him off.

He split me with the broken coffee mug to the tune of eight stitches. I think I was 13 at the time. He would not drive me to the hospital. My mother could not drive then, hadn't taken lessons yet, so me and my mammy walked to the bus stop and waited for the Number 5 bus. My arm wrapped in a sheet, covered in blood.

I don't know what lies she told the doctor at the hospital. Whatever it was, they bought it. They were not as strict back then about domestic abuse.

My father was a man consumed by duty and ambition. I could sit next to him in a vehicle and ask a question about anything. He would not answer until the gears in his head lowered the question to the level upon which it should be answered. Ever heard the line "excuse me, I've got a bigger name on the other line"? This was before cell phones. He did it all in his head. A man completely oblivious to all except his own agenda. He was not a dad. He was my own personal computer. Before they were invented. I was ignored. Not ignored, but an aside. I think my father equated no criticism as praise. Foolish man, but a product of the time. The Second World War has a lot to answer for, yet undiscovered.

Hell, I was no angel. I stole shit, shoplifted, petty shit. Vandalized buildings. I was an avid paint sprayer. One of the first, I say proudly. But I was a good kid at heart. I'd stand on the bus to give cripples and pregnant women seats. I'd help old ladies across the street. Up 'til then I was not a bad kid.

Then, around fourteen or fifteen, I started going to football matches and because I went to a Protes- tant school, I was a Rangers supporter. And an idiot. At around this time, I had not seen my father for at least a year. I mean not even glanced at him. Literally. He was up before me to go to work, left before I went to school and came home late, after I was in bed. An ambitious man. Absolute truth. I did not lay eyes on him for over a year. We lived in the same 3-bedroom, 1-bath apartment for a year without seeing each other. Seven of us. Unfuckinbelievable.

However, we did feel his presence. He put a lock on the fridge and a lock on the living room door. I would wait in my bed almost every day to hear the milkman deliver the five pints of milk we ordered every day. This would be about 5 am. At first clink, I was up and at 'em like a shot to the front door. I would down one full pint of creamy goodness in about 10 flat. Throw the evidence, the bottle, into the bushes outside my window and sneak back into bed. So much for your lock …DAD! FU

All the years I knew him he made me uncomfortable, like he hated me. I don't say that lightly, he really made me scared. I must have disappointed him greatly. I wonder if he had similar issues with my granddad. Anyway, over the years he managed to get rid of all his friends for one frivolous reason or another. I wonder if he had something to do with that. Hmm? Or was it me?

I was probably the first child he'd ever met. Except for my poor cousin Alice. She was nine months older than me. A "Special" girl. By all accounts he was really good with her.

It was rumored she was dropped on her head at birth. Sounds like the start of a joke. It's not. She had all manner of problems at birth. Bad eyes, couldn't hear well, she generally acted like a Downs Syndrome kid without the "look."

I, on the other hand, was a normal, adventurous mommy's boy who liked the status quo. The status quo being, me, the center of the universe. So I kinda resented this overgrown boy scout who's cramping my style and distracting my "Ladies" from me. Looking back, I make my father sound like an ogre. What he really was, was an unconsciously funny guy. Hardworking, ambitious and smart in an unedu- cated way. Oh! He knew his 3 Rs and read up a storm but in a scattered manner. Like me. But I suppose that's what happens when it's your opinion. And only yours.

Both he and my mother were not at home one day. Unusual for her, though not for him. I was fucking around with some bleach in the living room where he had just installed a brand new Axminster woolen fitted carpet with a very modern, sophisti- cated, criss-cross pattern.

He was very proud of this red and green fitted beauty. Even I knew it was expensive and that's why I'm sure it was "blagged" – stolen – to you unsophisticated non-Glaswegians.

I'm sure it had fallen off the back of a lorry at some point. Anyway, while I was playing with bleach in the living room. I SPILLED SOME. IN THE FUCKING LIVING ROOM!!!

What the fuck you doing with bleach, let alone in the living room?

Don't ask me why I was playing with bleach in the living room. Just let it be said I SPILLED SOME. Some right in the center of the room on the red and green woolen source of pride. Jesus H!

I immediately soaked it with water, so it went unnoticed for weeks. I don't know how I knew this was the right thing to do. If only temporarily.

One day, coming home from school, he was there early and conducting one of his frequent inquisi- tions. "Who spilled bleach on the carpet? The rug had begun to fray. "Well, who did it?" he bawled to a terrified audience of children. This was a rhetorical question at this point. He had already made his mind up it was Linda, the oldest girl and my best friend at the time. Linda couldn't outlast this onslaught, so eventually she gave me up. "It was Jim, daddy. He did it. I told him not to," she cried.

Bitch had grassed me. That means ratted me out. Now I'll get it. I went bright pink, so he knew she wasn't lying. I waited for the back of his hand. It never arrived. He was too stunned. Instead, he spun on me and said one of the funniest lines I've ever heard.

"When you get older, if you make it that far, and you buy your own house, I'm going to sneakily break into your nice new house and do a big shit right in the middle of your living room carpet."

His face was apoplectic and the reddest red I'd ever seen until he realized what he'd said. He looked at my mother. She was halfway to a smile. They both turned towards the door and wheeled out, closing the door behind them and into the hall, howling with laughter.

We children were so relieved we howled too, but mostly with relief. I had dodged a bullet.

Nothing was ever said about the accident ever again. Ever. But later that night, I caught my mother and father exchanging glances and smirking at each other. I'm sixty-nine now and I have forgotten their age at the time. I would be eight or nine and they were not even thirty. Barely adults living an almost hardscrabble life and trying to figure out what to do with all of these boisterous kids. It must have been stupid hard. We did not make it any easier.

2

PERVERSIONS & DIVERSIONS

We moved from Partick to Castlemilk when I was about five, to my first school, Castleton. I don't recall too much about Castleton but I do remember a couple of things.

Castleton would have been described in brochures at the time as a Post Modern Primary School set amid the hills just outside Glasgow, intended for use as an entry into the great Universities of Scotland.

In reality it was a two-story slum that was two years old and already showing signs of age. There were fifty kids in my class of 1958. This does not mean the same in Scotland as it does in the US. Class, in Scotland, means classroom not year. The classrooms were designed for twenty to twenty-five kids and fifty were crammed in. Not a great start to one's education, but typical of Britain just after the 2nd World War.

A couple of things I recall about Castleton are "running a race in the schoolyard" and "displaying body parts." Not sexually of course. I was only five for heaven's sake.

I remember the race so well because I went straight through the finish line and straight through the plate-glass window and onto a classroom desk. The race was run in the schoolyard, a concrete slab that ran the length of the building.

Lined up at one end were seven or eight guys just before the grass edging started. The race was started by one of the girls. Ready, Set, Go.

I led from the start and right behind me was McFadyen, who was becoming my arch enemy. The finish was whoever touched the wall of the class- room first. Just as I was about to declare victory, I felt a little nudge.

I was on a desk, not a mark on me, feeling pretty good. A little strange. "On a desk?" I had just won, when I felt a tug.

It wasn't the going through the plate-glass that caused the injury. No damage going in… it was pulling me back out over shards of glass sticking straight up. That was the problem. "My Lord, he's gonna die!" Not comforting words from the school nurse as she fanned herself with an empty hand.

The assistant nurse nearly fainted, my teacher swooned, the Headmaster harrumphed and Sinky, the janitor, the only sensible person there, grabbed a bandage.

"Gimme the effin' thing," he commanded.

He stopped the bleeding and called the real nurse, who came and quickly, if clumsily, stitched me up.

Looking back, I *could* have died if not for Mr.

Sinclair, Sinky, the janitor and resident pragmatist. They all nearly had a collective coronary. Except for Sinky. My wrist was spewing blood. Quite a little fountain, as I recall. I did not cry as you'd think a kid of five would've. There was no pain, or very little. I have a scar on my wrist, which even today is visible at midnight. The nurse must've been an apprentice or a rookie because I can still count stitch marks on my wrist after sixty-four years.

Fifteen stitches, if you must know. This is one of the reasons I've always had an affinity for practical men. Don't blather about it. Do something, even if it's wrong.

My other memory is Wullie Brown challenging me to "show bums." This was the height of naughti- ness. Wullie Brown was in my class and lived with seven other brothers and two sisters the next building over. He was a naughty kid who liked to do anything in class except learn. He was three feet four inches of mischief. If a spitball was fired. It was Wullie. If somebody was caught trying to see girls' knickers. Wullie would be in the mix somewhere. Naughtiness personified.

"Hey Jim, fancy showing bums?" enquired Wullie Brown, the local daredevil.

"Whit fur?" said I. Why?

"Ah don't know. See if yours is diff'rent," ventured Wullie.

"Whit if it is?" I asked. "Well, mines is the same as ma mammy's. Only smallur," I put forth.

"Yoo seen yir ma's bum?" Wullie asked, wide- eyed.

"Aye, yoo huvnay?" Deep conversations when you're five.

"Fuck naw. Ma da wid kill me," Wullie stated with certainty.

"How dae ye know?"

"Cos ma da caught Nigel sneekin' a peek. An' gave him a right good leatherin'."

Nigel was Wullie's older brother and a notorious peeping Tom. He was eleven years old and been caught more times than Harvey Goldstein trying to "perv" the local lassies. And mothers.

"Ah know who ye are, ya dirty wee swine." Was not an uncommon echo around our backyard. Anyway, what do you expect from a guy named Nigel? The Brown family did it to themselves was the common conclusion. Fucking Nigel! I ask you? Or as he's known these days, Councilman Brown.

But Wullie wasn't into that kind of thing. Nothing sexual. Wullie didn't know what sex was. Truth be told, I don't think much has changed. But this was very naughty, therefore, irresistible. It was late September when Wullie invited me to sho bums. The weeds were erect but dying. More like straw really.

The morning was crisp so I was a little reluctant to bear my bum. "Aw c'mon ya 'fraidy cat." The ulti- mate challenge to a five-year-old.

We stepped off the path to school, maybe six feet back and hunkered down in three feet of dried-up weeds and showed BUMS. We were big boys back then... WE WERE INVISIBLE... We were five.

～

I GOT MY FIRST KISS at Castleton. From a girl called Muriel McEwan. She was a plain little thing with a pinched face in a trench coat and beret. A beret! Oh my! In Castlemilk. Such panache.

That was an imitation of my mother, only she wouldn't have used "panache." Spoiled little bitch would be closer. Her mother always dressed her well. Every morning she was smart as a tart. Well, she was an only child to that point, so she should have been. According to my mother. There was plenty of back- stabbing and one-upmanship in the lower classes, even in a tenement town like Castlemilk.

I was walking to school one morning. It was November so it was gonna rain at some point today. I had to pass Muriel's flat to get to school and this particular morning she exited the "close," the entrance to the flats, just as I was passing. She looked very cute in that little beret. We stepped in line with each other completely unintentionally, but in perfect time, so it appeared to be meant.

Well, her little friends, seeing this could only whoooo and point. I was challenged again. Shades of Wullie Brown. I reached over and almost kissed her lips. I missed by one lip-width, but that was enough for her three little buddies to giggle all the way to school.

Another recollection was an unslakable desire to learn. I was curious about everything. To this day I can recall my little pink spelling book. "I" before "e" except after "c." And other immortal phrases. It wasn't even a book, it was barely a pamphlet but I memorized those words from back to front. I got a prize for coming in first in the class.

"Hey Jim! How dae ye spell kwasong?" says he, tittering with his buddies. Fucker meant croissant. That was Tommy McFadyen. "Fucking poof!" My arch enemy.

He beat me at a test, once. Wasn't about to forgive that.

McFadyen! sssppew! What a homo.

"Same as yer ma spells douche," I stabbed in return. What a retort. Need to file that away for future comebacks.

Bastards knew I couldn't speak French. Nobody could speak French. Fuck! The French barely squeezed out a word. Everybody knew the French spoke by pursing their lips and shrugging their shoulders.

I must have been an obnoxious little shit surrounded by other obnoxious little shits back then. I was first overall, not just in spelling. Arithmetic, no problem. I had reached my nine times table! History? No sweat.

At the battle of Culloden. "We had beat the English."

But nothing to do with school. And of course. Soccer. Again, "We had beat the English." Was there no end to my expertise?

Of course, there was a limit on the money for the first prize and my request for an encyclopedia exceeded this limit.

I heard the teachers talking. So sweet. They agreed to kick in the additional coin for my prize. I was so proud. I WAS WORTHY. Things like that stay with you the rest of your life.

～

NOT MUCH TO SAY ABOUT the rest of my days at Castleton except for one incident I recall. When my mother sent me for the "messages." That's Glaswegian for shopping.

I was about six or seven years old and was becoming stronger, physically, each day. My mother entrusted me with a list and ten shilling note to buy some groceries. Included in the list was a stone of pota- toes. A stone is fourteen pounds. That and the rest of the shopping was quite a weight for a seven-year-old.

I secured the "messages" and managed to get home feeling very proud of the weight I'd carried. I just reached my close (entrance to the tenement building) when the change from the ten shilling note slipped out of my hand. I managed to find all of it except a half a crown. Two shillings and sixpence. That was a shitload of money to my mother back then.

It had been snowing, and the coin had fallen in a little drift and was lost. I looked for a long time. Couldn't find it. I dragged the groceries upstairs and explained to my mother what had happened. She slapped me. First time she had ever hit me. I cried and ran into the bedroom. I felt like shit and I think she did too. I hugged my dog Shadow for a long time that day. He was my best friend and always forgave me. He was a Border Collie. I brushed him every day so his coat was an oily sheen. I loved him almost as much as my mother.

From feeling so proud of myself for carrying out this arduous task, this magnificent feat of shopping, to this ignominious defeat was almost too much to bear. I hated my mother and loved her with my whole heart all at once. That was real conflict for a wee boy my age.

Five months later I was passing the same area where I had dropped the change and thought, "I should take a look for that half crown."

The snow had melted by then and some grass had begun to grow. Of course, there was no chance it would be there. I walked over to the area where I'd dropped it, kicked over some grass and there it was. Holy heather!

I picked it up and ran as fast as I could to show my mother. I thought briefly about keeping it but the joy it would bring to my mammy was too sweet not to see.

Even then my larceny was beginning to peek through. I was a little miscreant in the making. Though I was hardly Al Capone, I was kind of a Disney version of Bugsy Siegal.

I found her at home and gave her the coin. I was expecting rapture, untold joy, but encountered subdued pleasure. When I look back I think she, while happy about receiving the money, (you could feed a family for a half crown back then) remembered she'd slapped me and her regret spoiled whatever joy the money might bring. That's the story I'm telling myself anyway.

Temptation, the desire to please, love, all conflicted and were just beginning to be recognized as separate emotions in my head.

Doing right, even seeing the difference between right and wrong. A nascent recognition of sin without the benefit of religion. That's what I would have thought. If I had learned to think by then.

3

WATER, WATER EVERYWHERE & PLENTY OF TIME TO THINK

From Castleton, I was wheeched away at age eight to mysterious Tormusk, a school very close to the Cathkin Braes. My playground when I was a kid.

To let you understand, Glasgow sits in a valley between two sets of hills, Cathkin Braes and the Campsie Hills. About twenty-five miles apart and bisected by the River Clyde.

There's a saying in Glasgow that if you are standing on the Campsie Hills and you can see the Cathkin Braes, it's going to rain and if you can't see them. It's raining.

In Glasgow it rains, on average, about 300 days a year. It's the only place I've ever been where it doesn't just rain straight down or horizontally. A lot of places claim that, but even if you're looking down, it'll bounce up and hit you in the face. Vertical rain, straight up.

It's my opinion that this has led to the screwed up, puzzled look on most Glaswegians' faces. Not only because we're squinting to avoid the rain but we're wondering what in Jesus' name is the rest of the world thinking. You acquire this look in Scotland at an early age. It never really goes away.

I have a vague recollection of my first day at Tormusk. I looked good…. ish. My shorts were that woolly kind that itched like pepper in your pants. My shirt was Rayon, that shit that catches fire if you rub it too fast and I wore an equally itchy jacket with a rope strung through the sleeves with two gloves attached. And a woolen cap that itched. And socks. That also itched. I was just itching to charm everybody.

I'd like to say I made an entrance. So I'm glad I said it but it wasn't true. I was eight when I arrived at Tormusk and twelve when I left and I don't remember learning a damned thing, consciously. Except, those little girls and that kiss.

Tormusk School was a refuge from the numbing boredom which was Castlemilk, the suburb where I lived. There wasn't even a street sign to distract you from the dullness. Those signs you see on motorways and highways would've been considered decorations in Castlemilk. Not blight. So Tormusk was a great distraction. I enjoyed both my teachers and classes. And of course, the Cathkin Braes. And the stories.

Here's one of my favorite stories. The wee green ball. A classic.

It's been so long I don't remember if this was a joke or it actually happened. Anyway, one morning there was an interruption in class, tables scrapping on floors, murmurs of disapproval from the kids. Finally, the teacher says, "What's going on?"

Charlie Findlay was an oddity. Smart as a nippy sweetie. (Spicy candy) and dumb as a rock, simulta- neously. He was tall. Very tall, five feet nine inches at 10 years old. He never had any money and had bucked teeth and was skinny. People joked he was so skinny he only needed one eye. But he had more balls than a brass monkey. There he was on his hands and knees feeling around on the floor between desks and chair legs looking for something.

"Charlie! What ARE you doing?"

"Looking for my wee green ball, Miss Jackson." "Oh! Get up. Let's have a look." She then proceeded to march over to the area, shoved aside a couple of desks and peered at the floor, moving chil- dren and chairs aside to find the elusive wee green ball. Pretty soon all the kids in the class were searching. Pushing and shoving.

"Move it."

"Fuck off." "Who said that?" "There it is."

"No it's not."

"He's touching me!" "That was my finger."

"I hope it was a Number Two pencil, McCartney," says Miss Jackson. Miss Jackson was anything if not precise. "I've got my eye on you. Buckster."

After about five minutes of this Miss Jackson had had enough and remarked, "Sorry, Charlie. Looks like it's lost. Must have fell down the ventilator grate." Charlie sighs, reaches up to his face, sticks his finger up his nose, pulls out a snot and declares, "It's ok, Ma'am. I'll just make another one." He proceeded to roll another "wee green ball."

Well, bedlam followed, coupled with disgust. The boys thought it was hilarious and the girls thought it was hilarious AND disgusting. From that day on, Charlie was my hero. Who was touching who and whose finger was the culprit was never discovered.

I was there for four years and don't remember much but I do remember the "Exam."

That's when Scottish education takes a wrong turn. They send the clever fuckers to "Senior" secondary schools and the dumbshits to "Modified" secondary schools. There should have been an avenue for "Salvageable douchebags" and another for clever but "Ultimately Save-able." Just 'cause you were slow to reach their arbitrary standards, this did not make you "wrong" or stupid.

You sat an "Exam" called the 11 plus. This exam was an indication of how clever you were and went a long way to determine which Secondary school you attended. You sat this exam during normal weekdays but it was a full day event if you needed it and was proctored by teachers from other schools. You could leave whenever you finished answering the questions but not before. It was as formal as I ever saw 'til this time.

Everybody dressed in school uniform. Charlie showed up late, dressed as a clown. At least that's what it looked like. We later found out he had been up all night with his dad, mom, three sisters and four brothers, moving furniture so they could escape paying next month's rent. They emptied their apart- ment because of poverty.

Charlie fell asleep in the back of the truck with all of their furniture and his sisters decided to apply makeup to poor Charlie, then quickly woke him up and chased him off to school.

Charlie knew nothing about this and tried to make it on time to Tormusk to sit the most important test of his school life. I sometimes wonder how old Charlie did in life. Maybe he became a clown? But I'm leaning strongly towards politician.

This test would forever brand you as an idiot or a genius. I was a clever little fucker back then. In a class of thirty I was either second or third in the class. Every year. Never made 1st though. Brian Hendry was first. Always. Prick! But, I always liked Brian. He was a decent footballer, unlike me, and an adventurous kind of guy. Like me. We both went to (or were sent to) "Bogie" Strathbungo Senior Secondary School and just kind of drifted apart. He did go a wee bit odd after his dad died.

His father died when he was twelve, of kidney failure, I think. His dad never qualified for treatment on the newly invented dialysis machine. Dirty rotten fucking shame. I liked his dad. I saw him on his bed wasting away in a two-bedroom, soon to be hovel. Not even in a hospital. Bastards. He qualified for me. Brian wept like a little kid when he was telling me his dad had died.

I remember being surprised at the crying and thinking "We're big boys now. We don't cry." You don't cry from physical pain, at least I don't, but you soon find out there are many more things in life that can cause you hurt worse than any corporeal crap. That was one of them.

My time passed quickly at Tormusk. I just went about my days, not actually doing great stuff. Just thinking about soccer, talking the usual crap about sex and football. Then sex and money and their great ability to connect at this level and then sex and money and manipulation.

I was a wiseass by then and knew everything, twice. Slang in Glasgow at the time for a smart-ass was "Wide." They called people like me "Double Wide." I wasn't. Far from it, but that was my rep then. Wee Raymond Markowitz was my classmate then. A short Jewish guy in my class. He was getting bullied. There was no understanding of bullying when I was a kid in Castlemilk. You either did or did not. Not to oversimplify but in our reptile brain, it goes Food... no food. Fear... no fear. Pain... no pain. That was the extent of our capacity. You knew something was not right. Just didn't know what. I knew what was not right.

Poor wee Rammie was getting pushed around by eejits (Irish slang for idiots). So I decided to stop it. I walked behind wee Rammie going home one day and caught these two eejits ruffling his hair, forcing his books from his hands to the mud.

I grabbed both by the neck and said very clearly in their ears, "Leave the wee guy alone." Didn't hit them. Didn't really assault them (by the standards of the time) but they got the message. So did I. There was right and there was wrong. I was big and I could fix some of it. But like most kids of 10, I got half the message.

∽

THAT'S ABOUT THE TIME I went to Strathbungo. Bogie to the initiated.

That's when I met Isabel. She was a beautiful girl about five feet six inches tall with short, wavy, red hair and green eyes, a wide mouth and full lips. She laughed loudly and often. Even at my jokes. She had long shapely legs which she showed to great advan- tage wearing mini, even micro skirts and stiletto heels. Heels were not in style at this time but she just knew what would turn heads.

What WAS in style then were suspender belts (garter belts to you yanks) and stockings. She wore those a lot and if the need arose to bend over to pick something up? She'd take it. My mouth goes dry just thinking about her.

She was just a smidge smarter than me. Now, when I say smidge, I mean the distance between me and Mars would have been closer. And I thought she was Pollyanna personified. Okay, I know Pollyanna was a person so therefore did not need to be "Person- ified." I meant I was enamored. Smitten. Like a feline is smitten with catnip. And prim. How could anyone who looked like and acted like her be so proper?

So prim, her ass genteelly squeaking when she sallied back and forth. At least I hope it was a squeak. And I can assure you she sallied a lot, in my mind, at night. Lying on my bed. I could only imagine what was happening between those thighs and gusset. So, instead of imagining, I produced the quintessential movie drama thought process in my head. In other words, I went insane. I fell in love. Didn't just step in it. Fell in it. Like normal folks? Nope. Not Ole Howdy Doody goofy smile aw shucks Dumb Shit bowel movement would do. Noooooosssiiiirrreeee. I dived in it.

Wallowed in it swam in it. And convinced myself she deserved it. I could see hyacinths, smell tea tree bark and whiff the essence of Fudulence. (Fudulence has no meaning except to me and it will stay that way.) But no hint of treachery or subterfuge… yet. You need to get a little older to suffer those two beauties.

Her name was Isabel Murdoch and I thought she was gorgeous. I loved her then and I think I still do. We were young sixteen, seventeen maybe, so it sounds like puppy love. It wasn't puppy love for me. I fell hard for that wee girl, but she didn't for me.

To this day I think about her. Her laugh, her femaleness. I don't remember her smell, but I do her presence. I remember her being close to me, like it was yesterday, the essence of her like a hot wet bath of oil.

She dumped me for a would-be gangbanger. I was crushed and being seventeen, I wanted to hurt her. Instead, I just cried.

At seventeen years old she was the epitome of my life. So sad I will never see her nor that time again. I didn't realize it then but she was keeping me out of jail. My friends were all working-class kids with the usual adolescent tendencies to vandalize and shoplift. When we split, I hung around with my buddies more and got up to more mischief and encounters with the law.

One of these encounters was pretty serious.

G.B.H. Grievous Bodily Harm. The next charge up was Attempted Murder so I knew I would get some time behind bars.

4

THE LAWYER, THE BITCH AND HIS WARDROBE

I showed up at court for sentencing with my granny Findlay. She had volunteered because my mother couldn't make it, having the rest of the kids to look after. I knew I was in trouble in court when the judge told my lawyer to get his feet off the court's chair.

"Mr. Vinegar," the judge said to my lawyer. "Would you be so kind as to remove your foot from my chair please?"

"I'm sorry, your Honor," groveled my young, incompetent, slightly disheveled apprentice lawyer.

Mister Lionel Vinegar, my lawyer, was an untidy man who wore a frock coat, skinny trousers, gaiters and a high collar shirt tied with a loose neckerchief.

He had been an apprentice lawyer for eleven years. At thirty-four, he was the oldest Understudy in the system. Not because he was unintelligent. The opposite, in fact. He was too smart. It was rumored he was autistic but no test had ever been administered so it remained a rumor. He had a hooked nose on which balanced "granny" spectacles. This gave him the look of a man of fifty. If you can imagine him with a scuffed and bent stovepipe hat, you'd have the "Artful Dodger" grown old and decrepit.

"Thank you," sighed Her Honor.

She was a prize. An example of affirmative action, before the phrase was thought of, if I ever saw one. Skirt too short, makeup applied in layers, lipstick as red as a baboon's ass and an air of superiority. She was flirting with the clerk of court. The only thing that seemed to distract her from her amorous inten- tions was Mr. Vinegar's feet and where they were positioned.

My counselor duly removed his foot and proceeded to expound on whatever blather he was blathering on about. Nobody was listening. And pretty soon, during his diatribe, he forgot about the foot thing and did it again.

"MR. VINEGAR! MY CHAIR!"

Mr. Vinegar nearly had a stroke. I just shook my head. There was no jury. I was there just to be sentenced. So there was no need for this idiot to be giving us his best Perry Mason.

He rushed through the rest of his presentation. Got my name wrong. Explained that I was sorry for stealing the loaf of bread. That I needed it to feed my family. What a screwup.

Well, not really exactly how it went, but you get the drift.

The judge became serious. Just before this she was yukking it up with the clerk of the court. Then she said… "Oops."

"Ahem! You have pleaded guilty to a very serious crime in which a loaf of bread was…."

"What?" The judge leaned forward to hear the clerk. "The other one, Agnes," the clerk whispered.

"Ah yes, you have pleaded guilty to a very serious crime in which a young man was… Stabbed?" The clerk nodded, smiling.

"Society cannot tolerate…blah blah blah." I could've sentenced myself with more decorum. What a bitch.

I was sentenced to be remanded in an Approved School of the Department's choosing for the term of one year.

My wee granny was crying and I felt like shit. She was a tiny person. Four feet ten inches and 97 pounds wringing wet. There's one of those pains you suffer that isn't physical, except it is. I felt like weeping myself but big boys don't cry, remember.

She approached Mr. Vinegar still dabbing her eyes. "What happens now, Sir," she whispered.

"He'll be taken to the cells to await placement in an institution as ordered by the court," Mr. Vinegar pronounced. I would have thought it heartless, what he said, but having spent some time with "Ole Lionel," I found it easy to forgive. There was some-thing not right about that boy. He turned to me. "Docherty, this is step one for you. If you don't get away from Glasgow and the people you think are your friends, you'll end up here, in and out for the rest of your life. Don't be a mug."

Ole Mr. Vinegar was not so dumb after all. I was a smart ass. Too clever by half and considered myself a fount of knowledge but one thing I never thought I was....was A MUG. That one stung. I kissed my wee granny and told her everything would be ok.

My wee orange-u-tang. I had hurt her and that's when I cried.

~

LET ME EXPLAIN HOW WE got to this point. We went, me and the other adolescent jerk-offs I hung out with, to a party way out of our territory. Just asking for trouble when I look back on it now.

We took the bus to Springburn, a suburb of Glas- gow, about fifteen miles away on the other side of town.

We lived in Castlemilk. A delightful fishing village on the Clyde. A slum. Well, it wasn't really a slum. I'd like to say it was a slum but in reality, it was a slum waiting to happen. Not a real slum, a pre- pubescent, unripe, proto slum. And we were the plants which would grow from this manure.

Glasgow city elders should be ashamed of them- selves. We were raw but clever, moldable, creatures.

They saw us as peons. Creatures of limited intelli- gence only fit as drones harvesting the crops for the elite. Who happened to be English and spoke via the right accent.

I don't know how word got around that six of us were having a party with the local girls in Spring- burn. But it did and soon the entrance to the "close" was surrounded by at least fifty or sixty gangbangers throwing rocks, bricks anything they could get their hands on to try and smash the windows. They succeeded. Not just the glass was smashed but the astragals, the wooden cross bars, were broken too. As well as the TV and other bits of furniture.

We were lying in this room, cowering in fear, on the floor, for the best part of two hours before they finally left. This apartment was on the third floor so you got to admire their aim and their heaving ability to reach up there.

Nobody called the cops and the cops never showed. I found out later the cops knew but were too scared to intervene.

After lying there for hours, I was pissed and looking for revenge. I wasn't carrying a blade and nobody else was either, to the best of my knowledge. But I needed a weapon. These motherfuckers had just TD an entire apartment. Totally demolished. For two hours those bastards threw bricks and stones through the windows. I wanted to kick the shit out of someone. In a closet full of old junk I found a file, a rasp really, about 12" long. It had no handle, just a spike where the handle would fit. So I grabbed it and stuck it down my pants.

Then me and another couple of guys crept down- stairs. It was dark; they had smashed the light bulbs on each floor so it was pitch black until we reached the street.

My first thought was, let's get the fuck home, so we started toward the bus stop when I recognized Denny Gallagher. He wasn't with us but he came from our area. What the fuck was he doing here? Only one explanation. He had some connection to the gangs in Springburn even though he lived twenty miles away. This was the motherfucker who stirred the shit and got the locals all riled up.

I chased that asshole for a mile that night, finally catching him from behind. I stabbed him in the small of the back with that large file. The tang end that the handle normally fits over.

I didn't hang around. I just jumped on the next bus back home and thought nothing more about it until the cops knocked on my door the next night. I wasn't worried about Denny Gallagher, in fact, I didn't know if I'd managed to stab the son of a bitch until later when they charged me. He got three stitches. A fucking bee sting they made sound like the Texas Chainsaw Massacre.

My mother answered the door and immediately went into hysterics.

"What have you done?" she screamed.

I felt lousy. Not because I stabbed a guy but because I made my mammy cry. It turned out ok because later that night my father gave me one of my usual beatings because I made my mammy cry.

I must have made my mammy cry a lot back then considering the amount of beatings I got. When I think back, that's how I ended up with the eight stitches from the coffee mug.

So Denny ended up winning. He got three stitches and sympathy from everybody. I got eight stitches and a beating from my father AND twelve months in the Pokie. Fucking typical.

My mother was devastated. She told me years later it was the only time she saw my father cry.

I didn't see him cry. At that time, I might have given a shit.

Up to this point I had encountered a lot of love, especially from women and dogs. My dog had been run over by a speeding bus a couple of months prior, so I was learning love sometimes involves a lot of pain. Swings and roundabouts. Yin and Yang.

5

THE KIBBLE AND SOME BITS

That's how I ended up in The Kibble, an approved school in Paisley, for about a year. Approved school in Scotland is a kind of transition between paying a heavy fine and jail. Oh, I don't mean paying more money. It was incarceration but more like Juvie. With dormitories and schoolwork. In other words a holiday camp.

The Kibble was a great place. I mean it. Full of games and work and school. And, what every boy in there needed. A sense of discipline. Just kidding, of course we didn't need discipline. We were all inno- cent. Snigger!

We slept in dormitories, about five to eight kids in each room. We'd wake up in the morning, shuffle down to the gymnasium (They weren't real big on marching at this school. As they were at

another place I was invited to attend in the future),
for the head count. Then mosey to the dining room
for eats.

(They WERE big on the mosey). The food was
ok and there was enough to fill you. Don't ever
remember being hungry at The Kibble. Or bored.

There was always something going on. I was
assigned to the carpenter's shop. We did all of the
repairs around the entire school. This was my job
four hours a day. The other four to five hours were
spent in class studying English, Math and Geography, and in between there was table tennis. I
became pretty good at the sport. At the end of
my time there I was the best player in the school.
I also got three 'O' levels because they allotted
class time to the smart asses among us. 'O' levels
were attained by reaching a certain proficiency in
whatever subject you chose. You needed 'O' levels
to reach Higher levels. Higher levels were needed
to enter University.

I read "A Town Like Alice" by Neville Shute
for the English 'O' level exam. I also read some
of his other books. "On the Beach," "Pied Piper."
I remember them to this day. Kind of. Popular in
their day but a little dated now, I think. Almost
fifty-five years ago. A lifetime. Our teacher, Mr.

Turner, cut through the bullshit as he handed out the books to the class.

"The only dirty bits in the book are on pages 151 and 152," he suggested. "So, I suggest you read those pages, suggest you wash your hands, then continue reading from the suggested start. Page one," he implied, raising his eyebrow sagely. As if we were dummies. Which we were. But didn't know it.

He was an admirable man, Mr. Turner. He was tall, about six feet, and stocky and hairy. Rumor had it a chunk of his face was blown off in the war, but we never saw anything to confirm that, being that he always stayed in profile. Goofy shit. Don't know why I said that.

We didn't see it because he wore a full beard. He was also smart and tough. Just the kind of guy you needed in this place. Because every one of these cherubic little motherfucking fuckers in here would stab you in the neck if they felt like it.

Mr. Turner was too good for this place. He was one of those tough guys who would fight Goliath and cry for a wounded bird. Just a very nice Highland Gentleman. I heard he was also on the board that created the final exams for the 'A' and 'O' levels for Scotland. A credentialed man. He made an impression on me, Mr. Turner did. I admired him and if remembering someone lets them live a while longer at least in your head, I hope I did ok, Mr. Turner.

There was one day I recall when the results of the exams came in. He handed out the results, typed on a piece of paper, no words from him, just sitting, hunched over, pretending to glance at the scores as if seeing them for the first time, handing those "toxic" papers to their owners with a grudging "HHRRU- UMPH" when you tried to say thank you.

He was as proud as punch, but would never let you see it. Just a very nice man. I hope he had a happy life. I think he'd be over a hundred by now so I'm assuming he's kicked it. Doff my cap to thee, Sir.

There were quite a few teachers and staff, I'm sorry to say, whose names have slipped my mind, but there's a couple I recall.

Pinky was the cook. Her name was synonymous with pink. Everything she wore, lipstick, eyeliner, uniform. All pink. She was always nice and I don't know why I felt this ... I just got the feeling she was always flirting with us "inmates." She was short and fat and fifty. Kind to us "Unfortunates." When I was allowed on work release, I always came in later than the school was open. Pinky always made us late- comers sandwiches. Wrapped nice in cellophane and plated with some fresh milk and a piece of fruit. Nice woman.

It was winter and always dark when I'd get back to The Kibble from my work release. The front door was locked so I'd come in through the kitchen entrance.

The normally bustling kitchen would be empty and sometimes the dim light would play tricks with your vision. For instance, my first night returning home, I stepped into the kitchen wondering why all the countertops and tables were black, (I knew they were white) and shimmering.

I found out when my boots crunched. I'm glad cockroaches don't make noises. At least not with their mouths. The sound of those disgusting creatures crunching beneath my feet was bad enough.

The sound of death…. even from a single cockroach would be bad enough. A thousand would be Hell. I felt sorry a nice little woman like Pinky had to work in this dump.

One or two steps into the room and the insects cleared. Thank God. It wasn't a dirty kitchen. That's just the way commercial kitchens were back then. I worked in many high-end kitchens in London and on the Isle of Jersey. They were all the same. Don't know if it's changed. Probably not.

Another teacher I remember was Mr. Gardiner. He was the headmaster of The Kibble. A small round balding, ball of a man. With the requisite tufts around the perimeter of his noggin. He wore glasses and the year I knew him, Mr. Gardiner was having trouble with his teeth. Not the ones in his head. The ones that sat at his bedside grinning and mocking him all night long. Those little ivory bastards, ever hawing never jawing. He just knew he hated them. But couldn't live without them.

Bad enough trying to be taken seriously if you're bespectacled, short, fat and bald. Try that when you're also toothless. Not a winning combination. Life's no fun if you're gumsy. How many successful men do you know who are bereft of teeth? Okay, maybe Gabby Hayes but that's about it.

So, he would try and wear these ill-fitting dentures until he couldn't stand it, then he'd reach in his mouth, normally whilst striding as if he was late. He always seemed in a hurry to be somewhere. Odd?

He wore a three-piece suit and brogues and when he could stand the pain no longer, he'd grab the dentures, uppers and lowers, flick the saliva off them onto the floor or wall or you. He was an untidy man. He was a kind man, he had an

English accent, he spoke frightfully posh and had the manners of a pig.

But he genuinely cared about the boys under his control. I saw him in tears when he sent a kid onto the next step up in the penal hierarchy. To Borstal. The man was not pretending. He was weeping. Crying like a baby for the soul he'd lost.

I found out later he'd kept me there a few weeks longer than my release date because they needed some "stability" for the new kids coming in. I wasn't happy about that then. Now I get it.

∽

My time at The Kibble came to an end with only one other incident. "The Great Underpant Robbery." That's what started it at least.

We were startled awake one night to the godawful sound of an alarm horn belting out its song. It was the burglar alarm. A fucking burglar alarm in a fucking Approved School?

Granted, it was not hard-core time but we were all sentenced to a term of incarceration. Who would want to break in?

The sound woke the whole school. Flashlights. Guard dogs. The security guards on duty and all of the kids, some of whom were seventeen years old and big. I weighed 185 pounds, sixteen years old and I was not the biggest inmate by quite a few pounds. 185 pounds was over thirteen stones. Not a small guy by Scottish standards.

We were all up and angry. "Who the fuck you think you are? Breaking into OUR jail?" Yeah, yeah, dripping with irony.

Anyway, nothing was found except a broken window in the laundry room. So, everyone agreed to go back to bed and do a complete search in the morning.

In the morning a thorough search was completed and all that was found missing was some underwear. Tidy whities. This was around the time of the Great Train Robbery. 1967. The largest train robbery in Britain at the time. Twenty million pounds of used notes on their way to be burnt and untraceable.

Hence, The Great Underpant Robbery. Of course, they showed up later in a washing machine. The machine had broken down, so the inventory count was off. Who knew they would include underwear in an inventory count? I'd be angry if I found them. YUCCHH!

That would have been the end of it except for one thing. During the search a fight had ensued between the biggest guy among the inmates, the "Donner" (the Donner was supposedly the toughest guy in the place) and another high-ranked resident, my buddy, Frank. Who had taken umbrage at him pushing little kids around. Our Donner was Hendy.

Hendy, the Donner, was big, stupid and had a face full of zits. "Plukes" we used to call them. Not so friendly reminders of adolescence.

Hendy was aware he had them and it was one way to get under his skin. He was a surly mother- fucker and thick, therefore scary. Stupid people tend not to be reasoned with easily and this douchebag was a prime example.

"Hey, get yer big mitts aff the wee yins," said Frank.

"Who the fuck yoo talkin' tae, fuckin' eejit?" asked Hendy. Part time bully and full time wanker.

"Yoo, moonface." Not a bad, quick, comeback from Frank.

"I'll fuckin' mollacate yoo," shouts Moon-face/Hendy, and rushes at Frank. Mollacate was a Scottish term for "rip you limb from limb."

We had a lot of words for that back then. The English would have called us antisocial. Just saying. "We'll fucking kill you" didn't quite get it done for us. Too posh. We needed to add a little more embellish- ment to our insults and threats.

Now, I don't think Frank could've taken Hendy but he was no pushover, so the fight was broken up. Just some pushing and shoving, leaving a resentment simmering.

Frank was no angel, but he had a sense of right and wrong. Most of us did. And that, dear friends, is what allows me hope to this day. I met very few bad guys in the slammer. Oh, plenty of misguided and some even unlucky souls but not many evil mother- fuckers. Well, the umbrage that Frank took started a kind of civil war among the kids. There was us, the good guys on one side and the Donner and his henchmen on the other.

Nobody liked the Donner. He was big, sixteen years old, 250 pounds if an ounce, and a bully. I mean some of the kids in The Kibble were fifteen but if they weighed a hundred pounds, I'd be a liar.

Hendy, short for Henderson, was a typical twat. He'd never bothered me because he and his henchmen didn't quite know how to figure me out. They knew I was taking extra classes for 'O' levels. So, they were kind of intellectually intimidated. Only around six or eight were invited per year so you were special in a limited sort of way.

And they knew I could kick their ass at table tennis. There was a hierarchy at that game too. But he did shove the little new kids around. So, he was not highly regarded particularly among the teachers and even among most of the inmates.

There was a loose cartel of us older kids. The ones who'd been there at least six months. We had figured each other out. Knew what gangs we were affiliated with and had sorted out if we could get along or not.

Hendy had a similar thing going on with his henchmen, only he liked the old-fashioned way.

"Do as I fucking say, or I'll squash your sporran." Or words to that effect. So there transpired a kind of detente, a simmering kind of truce to see how things would break.

There was Hendy, his henchmen on one side. He was escorted around by about six boot lickers. Any one of whom would be kissing my ass without their champion Hendy.

And us. Six or eight of us including a vicious, stocky little son of a bitch called Eddie Toal. One of the truly evil motherfuckers I mentioned earlier. He looked like a white Mike Tyson without the whimsy. Something had been simmering for days. Even the teachers knew something was afoot. As Sherlock Holmes could have said.

We, the cartel, had decided to act. We'd had enough of this preening douchebag who wouldn't last five minutes with real tough guys.

Every night before dinner the whole school would gather for the evening count in the gym. That's when we decided to act. Me and Eddie Toal would go first. I would take out the Donner's #2, a kiss-ass prick called Commy. Short for Comstone. I didn't like him, and he was not fond of me.

Eddie and two or three other guys would take Hendy. The other wannabees were non-entities and could be ignored.

I went first, ran over, grabbed #2 by the hair and dragged him over to the wall bars and slammed his head. I didn't stop kicking him until the teachers pulled me off him. Eddie, it turned out didn't need any help. He just nailed Hendy with a punch his ancestors would have felt and kept hitting him until he was dragged off.

There was an investigation. The local police were involved as well as the Department of Prisons. After three days the conclusion was reached that Hendy had to go. The teachers had been chronicling his behavior for weeks. Not so dumb after all. All of us were interviewed one by one and given a stern lecture. No other punishment was required except Hendy. He had to go.

They knew who was the cause of the trouble. A pompous ass who was too dumb to know the shit he was stirring. He left The Kibble crying and so was Mr. Gardiner. Felt sorry for the old man. Didn't feel sorry for that wanker Henderson.

My time spent in The Kibble was rewarding but ultimately unsatisfactory because it was too easy for me. I think I would have been better off getting a short sharp lesson in a real jail.

As you will see later, I still thought I was The Shit. Too big for my britches and arrogant.

I would still have a couple of more brushes with the law before I was done. But I was learning. Kind- ness wasn't a weak emotion. You can be tough and kind and fair.

Being good was yet a reach, but I could feel it coming.

6

US & PUS

While I was in The Kibble they got me a job as a carpenter's apprentice on day release at a construction company called Watlings.

Watlings was a great place to work. They employed about sixty carpenters and at least another 300 men in various other trades. A big outfit for Scot- land. We made something new every day. Building huge concrete forms for flyovers for freeways all made of finished plywood that could've made fine furniture. You would think it would be rough plywood they'd use to pour concrete into but it's not. It's finely polished plywood. It would take fifty or sixty guys to lift one of these things and huge low loaders to ship them. We also made prefab houses, packing cases and anything else where two pieces of wood needed to be joined.

All this and building an open plan staircase made from Parana Pine. A notoriously difficult wood to work with. Gorgeous to look at but it would split at the drop of an eyelash and bend like a banana if you looked at it wrong-wise. I loved that job.

I was in training with an elderly gentleman called Walter. And a gentleman he was. Carpentry was his life. Never married. Thought about nothing except wood and how to join the pieces. He stood about five feet six, bald with round John Lennon glasses. He looked more like a school teacher than a carpenter. A very nice man nearing retirement who you knew would never retire. He would work at his chosen profession until he dropped. Just that kind of guy.

While we were working on this project he gave me a little row boat. Perfect in every way, clinker built. Each piece shaped, placed, glued and screwed. It was a perfect replica only 1/10th the size of life.

He built it at home in his spare time. It was beau- tiful. Stained and varnished. It shone like enameled oak. He tried to give it to me. I nearly cried at the kindness. I couldn't take it. I was homeless at the time and it was all I could do to get to work never mind humphing ornaments around. I thanked him sincerely and with as much emotion as befits a tough guy trying to become a man. He felt for me, I think. Tried to hint that it was ok to be tough and kind simultaneously. I think he helped. I've remembered all these years. That has to account for something.

Walter came to visit me in jail while I was awaiting trial. He told me he would speak to Watlings management about me returning to work if I got out. I never saw Walter again but he left an impression on me. That impression was kindness.

I was growing but not yet grown so I went back to the same shit I was doing before. Drinking, getting up to nonsense I should be ashamed of. And gener- ally fucking around the way I'd done since I discov- ered my parents were way more interested in each other than they ever were in me or my siblings. My parents were truly in love. And were clearly made for each other. Even after six kids, we could hear them fooling around in bed.

In fact, looking back, my siblings and me were all just an expensive annoyance, an irritation that had to be dealt with before they could get back to shagging each other. Maybe that was just my impression but it ended up being one that has lasted. Come to think of it, I've never really had a conversation with my brothers or sisters about our parents.

After a few wild months I ended up back in the slammer again. Only this was the real thing this time. Real honest to God prison. That was the end of Watlings.

Another assault. I got twelve months this time which meant I could be out in eight to nine months given time off for good behavior.

Went to Barlinnie. Was there about three months. It was like being back home visiting with friends.

Thieving, lying, conniving friends but friends nonetheless. Ashburn Findlay was one of these friends. A scalawag of skullduggery, a rapscallion in rudeness, a dastard of debauchery. All in all, a first- class wanker I'm proud to call my friend.

He was a handsome guy, Ashburn Findlay, in a fucked up, Paul Newman kinda way. And the mother fucker was tits up funny.

This was typical of our conversations in jail. I'm on the top bunk bed leaning over, talking to Ashy.

"Hey, Ash! Fancy going out tonight?" I'd whisper from my upstairs bunk in the prison cell. You had to whisper, the guards patrolled every fifteen minutes and they hated noise. So did the inmates. After all, when you're asleep, you're not doing time.

"Yeah! Man! Where ye fancy? Maryland?

Locarno?" (Local dance halls/discos.) "Nah. Too crowded," said Ashy. "Lindella?" I suggested.

"Too much pussy," he replied.

"Too much pussy?" Up until that point it had never occurred to me that there could be such a thing as "too much pussy." I must have been living a very sheltered life 'til that point.

"So, how 'bout just taking a wee donner (slang for a casual walk) down to the 'Kind Man' the local pub, have a few beers, stagger back home, crash on the couch and wake up feeling like shit?" I ventured.

"So when you put it like that... I think I'll just stay in tonight." So we decided just to stay in our cell again that night. Life is easy when you have no choice.

That was a sample of the deep conversations 'tween me and Ashy.

"Take a gander at this," says Ashy one night after work. Showing me a plastic pouch filled with what looked like snot and giving me a nudge.

"Blagged (Stole it) it fae the jinners' shoap." (Car- penters' shop (joiners/carpenters shop)

"Jinner's shoap?" I asked quizzically. "Whit is it?" "Aye, the nice clean room wi' awe the saws an' pliers 'n shit. Ye know, the wan wi' the tiles n stuff awe roon."

I nodded. "Ah ken where ye mean," I agreed. "It's glue, man. Get ye stoned, burlin' ye ken."

"Let's see that, ya dumpty." Dumpty was polite slang for fuckin' idiot.

He handed me the package. Purulent Exudate? It says.

"Whit the fuck's Purudanty Exudatey?" I enquired.

He shrugged.

"Ah don't know either but am no sticking that shite up ma nose."

We found out later it was Pus... Barfolomew. Real, honest to God, pus. The shit that oozes out of wounds.

Ashy had been on cleaning detail and one of the screws had taken him up to a floor he'd never been to.

It happened to be the Vivisection area of the jail. Supposedly long closed and forgotten. This was in 1968-69. You never know what goes on under the radar in the slammer. Well, do you?

Ashy had been left alone for a second and true to his nature, had dodged into an unlocked room, caught a glimpse of the tools and figured it was just a really clean carpenter's shop. Snagged what he thought was stoning material, got out and continued mopping.

He'd grabbed the "glue," stuck it down his pants and here we are. Thank Christ, I hardly touched it but Ashy had it down his pants for hours. Never saw a man scrub his balls so hard for so long.

I must admit I checked various parts of my anatomy for unusual growths for quite a few weeks after that.

Deep down there wasn't a lot of depth to Ashburn. But Ash was my friend for a couple of years and I thank him for it. I think he would think the same of me. Good guy.

Then I was gone from Barlinnie Prison. And make no mistake, it was a prison. Two walls made of stacked cells. Slap two end caps on the walls and drape a roof, install a central staircase rising to each ledge that connected each cell, multiply that six times, surround it all with a 30' high granite fence made of rough cut stones topped with barbed wire and you've got a prison.

∽

THEY SHIPPED US FROM GLASGOW, Barlinnie Prison to Edinburgh, in a single-decker bus with the chains round the ankles and wrists, the whole bit, to Soughton Prison.

Soughton was modern compared to Barlinnie. It looked more like a school than a prison but was infinitely scarier because of the newness. It made you feel they could keep you there indefinitely. They took us in the dead of day to no fanfare that I heard and no fireworks I saw.

Maybe this was when I started to get a clue that maybe my attitude was contributing to my latest run of "bad luck." Maybe I should try a different 'Tude. Anyway, this tousle-haired, sneering, over-the-shoulder Jimmy Dean look wasn't getting it done any longer. I was growing much taller, and broader to match, than my fellow ruffians. So I was going to be cool, OK?

No. Not too cool, though. I didn't want to have to stab my eyeball or kill some poor son of a bitch. Just cool enough to be considered possibly dangerous. Let's give it a go.

The bus from Glasgow to Edinburgh took about an hour and a half through beautiful countryside. Back then, Glasgow and Edinburgh were two well-defined cities. Now, it's hard to tell where one ends and the other starts.

We arrived at the gates. There were two of them.

Let us into one gate, closed it then let us through the other and closed it.

One screw (guard) entered the bus and unlocked us all. There were only six on the bus, all older than me. I looked at my fellow inmates. One in his mid- twenties, the other four in their fifties. Everyone a mess. Nobody looks good in prison stripes but these guys were pitiful. All needed a haircut and a shave. I hardly ever shaved, so a couple of days growth did not look amiss on me.

I said to myself, I've got to stop this bullshit. I don't want to be fifty and still doing this.

They lined us up outside the bus, checked our names off the list and marched us through to the Dog Boxes.

These were 1-man cells so naturally, they put three of us in one, threw in three sets of uniforms and told us to stuff our Barlinnie uniforms in a bag and wait. You're told to do that a lot in prison.

Four hours later we were let out and led to our cells. My cell was about ten feet by seven feet with a bed and small table and chair. It had a window six feet off the floor that had slats that were slanted up. You could only see the sky.

No books or magazines. Just a bible which I read until lights out. No food. We had missed dinner. Oh joy. Fell asleep until 6 am when lights came on signaling breakfast.

The next morning, we were ushered out to collect our assignments. The bible is the best-selling book of all time? Not if I was on the editorial board. You needed a helluva imagination to make the bible interesting as far as I was concerned. Like most things in jail, it was just boring. No torture. No fights. No threats. Just dull, which, given my personality, IS torture.

Anyway, I was assigned to the cobbler's shop as a "HEY YOU... YEAH YOU!! Do this, Wipe that, Kiss these." I thought that was my title for a few days.

What the hell I know 'bout cobbling? Well, it turns out, after a few weeks, quite a bit. I had actually re-soled and re-healed so many broken souls I was qualified enough to apply for sainthood. So I did pretty good at the ol' cobbler's shop.

I can't let the cobbler's shop pass without a mention of Ol' Watty. Mr. Watson, as he should be known. Because he was a Mister. A Gentleman, a gentle man from whom you got the impression he'd break your neck if you messed with him. He was a big dude who sported a pencil-thin mustache with a little twist at each end that made him look like Dick Dastardly.

He had a booming laugh and great teeth. Always wore a light-colored brown coat and a peaked cap with a badge on it that said Infinitum Illegitimi Carborundum on it. I found out later it was Latin for "Never Let the Bastards Grind You Down." He was English. And how he got to be a "screw" in a Scottish prison I'll never know.

He used to challenge us with general knowledge questions and brain teasers. Trying to keep us busy. He knew from first-hand experience, having dealt with so many souls, idle hands were the devil's playthings.

A clever guy was Mr. Watson. Read up a storm. Always curious about just about everything. He was retiring to Australia to be with his family. A daughter, I think. After forty years in the prison service he had come to realize the fault lay with the governors of the prison industry and politicians, not the misguided youth.

I have come to the conclusion, after fifty years of reflection, there were very few "bad guys." Just a bleating, power-hungry herd of politicians who had concluded their path to success rested on your neck. And "Woe betide" anybody who got in their self- appointed road to success.

I hope you had a happy life, my friend. You were kind to all of us. I also admired the way you conducted yourself with the other staff. Little jokes about saving souls with the chaplain? Eternally polite and a "Hail fellow, well met" type of guy. You were among us but only with us up to a point.

You still had to maintain discipline and you did so with humor and kindness. I liked you, Sir, and have remembered you for a lifetime. My little gift to you, acknowledging you long after your death. You deserved it, Sir.

∾

AFTER ABOUT THREE MONTHS I was transferred to the barbershop. I had applied for this transfer because it was the best gig in jail. Hair shampooed every day, learning shit that could actually be of help when you get out. They had classes that educated you. Clean clothes every work day. Shower anytime.

This was because we had to cut the hair of these filthy straggly mothereffers who the cops pulled in to dry out for a few days. So... Hell yeah! I'm in. A shower in jail is like a ten-minute vacation to the South of France and we could take forever if we wanted cos nobody wanted to go near these manky mofos 'cept us in the barbershop.

I actually passed some exams too, written exams. No really. I did. Additionally, I learned how to cut hair. A little.

Mr. Donaldson taught me how. As well as two convicted murderers. Peter Finnegan and Ronnie?? Don't remember his last name but he gave off this fucked up, evil vibe. Like Satan in a nice suit. Didn't trust that dude.

I remember Peter well because he was a very shy young man. He had murdered his girlfriend/fiancé because she was pregnant and he was raised by raving fanatical religious lunatics. They were hard-core Catholics by all accounts and I'll bet, fucking nuts. Not that there isn't any on the other side. There are some beauties out there too. Enough crazies to go around. If you ask me.

I never asked myself the ultimate question. Did she cheat on him? And he found out? Was this minor justification even a part of this deed? Or was it just a sex before marriage thing? I'll never know.

He had, he thought, strangled her. So he decided the best way to handle this was to bury her and his unborn child down by the canal. Problem was she wasn't dead. They found later she had inhaled dirt.

By this time I was becoming hardened, not to the point of indifference but getting close. Prison will do that to you, so sympathy for this poor girl was almost beyond my reach.

I think getting beaten a lot for shit I never did has something to do with it. Thank you, Mom. Not my father. He was just a puppet. Still harboring resent- ment, I see. Docherty.

If I was to guess, I think Peter will have been dead a long time now. He never appeared to me like he could have handled it. The killing I mean. I'd bet heavy he topped himself and I don't mean with sprinkles.

As for his parents doing a double homicide, your guess is as good as mine. But they should have. IMHO. He went to church a lot trying to repent, I assumed. If somebody was to ask me, I'd say they'd indoctrinated the boy and reaped what they sowed. My opinion only but you better learn to trust your opinion in the slammer because you sure as Christ can't trust anybody else.

The other murderer, Ronnie, I never really did know much about but I did hear he murdered his dear mother because she wouldn't give him money. Two shillings, I heard.

Even now I can hear the echoes from way back then where we should have seen this coming. This self-centered, self-absorbed, self-indulgent life we're living leaves a deal to be hoped for. As

I write, the future's not looking any brighter. That was a flash forward to when I'm writing this in 2021.

Oh, by the way, when Peter Finnegan was convicted, they used to prop a shovel against his cell door and sing "There was a man called Peter Finnegan, he dug a hole and filled it in again." This to the tune of some old Irish ditty.

Somebody would lean the shovel against the door. The screw who'd open the door would ignore the spade because nobody liked this guy or the screws were sadistic sons of bitches. (Well, they hated what he did, is more like what I mean.) Unlock the door and when Peter pulled it open it'd fall in with a helluva clatter.

My opinion, if he wasn't damaged goods before this, he sure as hell was afterwards. I got an inkling of what I had already suspected from my time with these two killers. Passion is great up to a point. Too much will kill you or get you killed. Circumstances be damned. It takes a certain kind of person to take another person's life. That person was not me. At this point I was kind of a badass but I couldn't do what they did. My time annoying the constabulary was drawing to a close.

~

PRISONERS ARE NOT KNOWN FOR their decorum. Peter was not a bad guy. I think he got a little fucked up by his folks. The irony is dripping. I spent six months working in the barbershop and learned a lot about life and a little about cutting hair.

I enjoyed the process of making someone look better and I enjoyed the schooling I got. Some things just stick with you. I remember the occipital bone, the short hair of the face and eyebrows and the name of the horribly nasty little beasties that live on our heads. Pediculosis Capitis.

Head lice. And Pediculosis Pubis. You can guess where they live. Take a wild stab. Pubis is the clue.

Our fearless leader in this enterprise was Mr. Donaldson.

Mr. Donaldson smoked too much, shook like a leaf, I'm assuming he wasn't a shaving dude, and was kind in the extreme. He tried to teach us about life and how to deal with people and their many splen- dorous fucked-up-itudes.

He was a real barber. Quiet when you wanted, gregarious when you approved, and always had those little accoutrements on him like a blackhead squeezer or a styptic pencil. He was a short, chubby, nervous little man who was cheerful at all times. I never really heard him speak. Everything was a kind of nervous twitter. He dyed his hair black and was very particular about his nails. Sweet man, I liked him and he liked me.

My time in Soughton was what I needed at the time. It showed me good dudes (there are as many in prison as there are on the outside) and some fuck- ups. Not bad. Just astray. And a few evil bastards.

You can spot them. They laugh at the wrong time. They don't say much. But they're always passionate about something. Could even be stamp collecting. You don't know. Watch out for the overen- thusiastic.

7
___

A LITTLE RANT ABOUT FAIRNESS, LAMENTING ITS RARENESS

R ight about this time I took a hard look at myself and didn't much like what I saw.

I was on the road to being a career criminal. I decided if I stayed in Glasgow I'd get into trouble again. I had already been huckled (nabbed, arrested) for several small-time crimes. Loitering with Intent, Disturbing the Peace. Petty Theft and the like. I had to get out of Glasgow. The people I was associating with were the problem.

Or maybe there was a flaw in me that felt the need to please these guys. To be one of the gang instead of having the balls to cut my own path. I wasn't a dummy but I was doing dumb things. Glasgow didn't help. The prevailing attitudes in Glasgow were gang related. Everybody my age was in cahoots with a local gang. And there were plenty.

There was a shit ton of gangs in the big city at the time. The result of government neglect. I'm not anti-government. Just anti-complacency. Whenever the people leave these fuckers (the bureaucrats) to their own devices they become corrupt. It's inevitable. And that, my friend, is the hardest part of being an adult. Knowing it is easy. Acting upon it is hard.

The Tongs, The Cumbie, The Pak, The Derry. Local gangs who filled a place where your father should have been.

I mean hundreds of gangs of young men growing up in a city that had industrialized the world but had forgot to include people. Made fortunes for the few but forgot indoor plumbing for the masses.

TV didn't help. California beaches and big cars. Seen every night but unattainable. If money was so important why didn't they teach us how to make it? Well, you know why. The Elite needed the Plebes to service them.

The 3 Rs were paramount in Scottish schools when I grew up. Then they fucked up and taught us Shakespeare and instead of Finance, Geography and History... and fucking Algebra.

These subjects should certainly be part of the curriculum but not given the importance they were. And today, are still not. Communism would be a great thing if it ever worked. It's also very pleasant to be served your morning tea by someone who could quote Shakespeare whilst kissing your ass.

All of the great inventions and movements were founded and created by men of leisure and the desire to pursue their inclination, not beating your-self twelve hours a day down a mine or working dawn to dusk to scratch a living on a subsistence farm.

Of course, hard work was important but not the kind of hard work you HAD to do. Where it was needed to put a crust in your mouth or a roof over your head. The kind you wanted or even desired to do. Or even, if you were lucky, driven by sheer compulsion.

If we are going to create a society that is built around money then teach us how to make it. Real money. Not this pissant, shit amounts that only allow for a nice car and a nice house but real money that allows for the pursuit of interests. Not piddling amounts.

When was the last course in school you heard of that taught anything about the stock market? Government? Insurance? At a meaningful age. That means early. Beginning when you were proficient at reading. If it was too early for you, fine. You'll get there in your own sweet time, if that was your jour- ney. But don't compel Algebra or Physics or even Chemistry. Teach a basic understanding that's sufficient.

Or fucking Languages. I took German for two years and French for three. Don't know shit about either. And never intend to. Der bliestift ist rot. I think that means "The pencil is red" in German. That's all I remember after two years? One hour per day, five days per week for two fucking years? You don't need Hitler to tell you something ain't right here.

The single most cost you will have in life is food. That's what you will spend most of life working for. The next? Insurance?

Insurance is not even given a mention in primary or secondary schools. That should have been my thoughts and attitude back then. It wasn't. I just knew instinctively I had to get out of a place that was a bad influence on me. Please don't think I'm bad- mouthing Scotland or even Glasgow. Or education.

But it just wasn't for me. There was a failure in me that didn't sit well with the prevailing culture in Glasgow. I didn't like being a criminal. But I was. Found no attraction to it. But was heading in that direction.

There was a desire in me to do good, be a better person than what I was so far displaying. I had no affinity for the Church. Didn't feel the need to pros- trate myself before God and beg forgiveness for my father's sins. Don't think so, Sunbeam.

I felt guilty enough about the shit I was pulling never mind paying for some other motherfucker's fuckups.

So I decided to go back to Newquay in Cornwall. I had been there four or five years earlier with the whole family for a camping vacation.

I called my buddy in Glasgow who I knew was having the same problems as me. Charlie Carmichael. Just like me, Charlie knew better. Just like me. He knew these people were out of step, wrong. Just like me. Charlie knew you could smoke weed and drink with no consequences. Just like me, he knew he'd be proven right one day.

And just like me, he was wrong.

But at this time we still had some wronging to do so he agreed to thieve some money from his mom's purse and come to Newquay to visit. Charlie was a small guy, blond and easily manipulated but a good buddy. Couldn't fight worth a shit but was handy with a blade. He was not bright but his family was rich, so what the fuck.

He arrived by train three days later. I had stolen a tent from an outdoor/expedition shop so we were all set to go camp. We chose the estuary. A sandy inlet near town that just begged for someone to camp there.

Newquay is a really nice town, coved beautiful beaches, each surrounded by 120' high unclimbable granite cliffs, nice hotels and gorgeous little girls away from home for the first time. Housekeepers, chambermaids, waitresses. All around eighteen to twenty-three years old. And adventurous. Especially in the late sixties, early seventies.

Hippy time, man, free love and smoking dope. I got hooked up with two nurses from London. One of them had a little crush on me. She never let me fuck her but she did enjoy stroking my cock. And, shock of shocks, I enjoyed it too.

We'd meet after she finished work and go forwalks along the beach until it got dark and the fami- lies left the sand, find a shadowy cove, and kiss for a long time while I stroked her thighs until she was ready to let me touch her slit. That was the signal for her to begin tossing me off. Which she did with prac- ticed hands. She was a nurse, for God's sake! She wanted to take me in her mouth but I couldn't let her and also couldn't tell her the reason.

It felt dangerous to me. The intensity would have made me faint. A big boy letting a little girl cause him to faint? Not happening, dude. Still plenty of the Presbyterian Glasgow left in me.

I did not work while in Newquay. I made money by ripping off the jukebox in a bar called The Sailors Arms. Very popular, jam-packed every night and everybody played the jukebox. Still there now, I believe. Saw it on Google Earth a few months back.

Every night I'd get in early, sit next to the jukebox, the side that had the reject button and the cup that held the coin when it was rejected. When I sat there it got rejected a lot. The machine was played so often you would never run out of songs, so nobody knew it wasn't their money that was playing a particular song.

I lived on that little scam for months. I was also up to no good early in the morning, robbing milk and groceries off doorsteps.

I got hassled by the cops all the time. After all, I was living in a tent on the beach with no known means of support.

I had pitched a tent on a sandy estuary outside of town. This was an area straight out of Treasure

Island. A sandy inlet with a 20-foot wide stream running through it and one foot deep at low tide. A little valley hidden from town by a low embankment on one side and a row of trees on the other. The entire estuary was maybe 80 feet wide at best and only flooded on spring tides.

The area was home to an old ship. A museum of sorts called "The Ship Ada" and ourselves. I'm using the Royal "Ourselves" here.

"Am goin' back tae Scotlan'" Charlie declared one day. This was after about two weeks in Newquay. But he said it with the same pronouncement as you would after a round-the-world voyage.

"Whit fur?" I asked. (Means why? in English.) "Ma mammy wants me tae help run oor shoap."

His family owned a flower shop in Rutherglen. A couple stores, I think they had.

"Ye don't like it here?" I enquired.

"It's no that. Ah think am homesick," he replied. "Said the exact same thing tae ma mammy one day," said I.

"Aw aye? Whit did she say?" he asked, lifting his eyebrow.

"She said, 'this is your home.' An' ah said 'Ah no. Am fuckin' sick o' it'." We giggled a bit.

He left soon after. His mammy had sent him

train fare. Didn't hurt he slipped me a few shillings before he left.

I liked wee Charlie and we left on good terms. He was just destined for another path.

～

THE SHIP ADA WAS AN old clipper ship blackened with age that just screamed Cutty Sark. It had washed up on the sand off to the edge of the estuary and just lay there, I suppose for years. It had been propped up with support timbers to keep it from keeling over at low tide.

It was still open as a kind of halfhearted museum and had been so for decades. It was maybe 75' long and skinny the way those old "tea clippers" were. It just sat there doing nothing for years. Not aban- doned. Just forgotten.

The sails, or sheets, were intact and furled when I was there. Me and Charlie ventured inside a couple of times down a narrow spiral staircase, and were greeted by lots of little ornaments from all over the world and a white-haired, wrinkled old dude. This dude was not wrinkled in the way you're usually wrinkled. This guy had vertical wrinkles. Wrunkles would be a better word. Like somebody had furled then unfurled him. Strange

looking old dude. Never saw him in our previous
visits to the ship. He wore a striped nightgown and
a long stained beard, like he smoked. But he didn't.
I knew this because he was balancing an unlit pipe
from his lips.

"Heyllo," he tried.

"How's it goin n'nat, know?" I tried back.
Thought I'd try a bit of Glaswegian on him since he
didn't seem too sure of the English language either.

"Whit?"

"Ah said 'How 'ur ye do-in'?" A wee bit hesitant.
"Fine, fine," says he, starting to get the hang of it.

"Don't get too many visitors these days."

"Don't suppose ye wid, whit wi' livin' on a
fuckin' wreck," I ventured. Me and Charlie giggled.

"Whit?" he enquired again.

"Place is a wee bit run doon, don't ye think?"
"OHH, Yes. Yes. Yes. It's been a while since the
maid paid a visit," he cackled. "Yes, quite a while."
Looking off at some distant horizon.

"So where'd ye get aw this crap?" That was
me being sophisticated. While sweeping my hand
towards a heap of semi-displayed clutter. Though
not your regular shit. It was different.

This was not your crappy plastic shit from
Hong Kong, (Hong Kong was known in Britain at
the time as the producer of endless plastic shit that

filled "Lucky Bags" and their ilk) but real genuine crappy shit from India and southwest Cornwall and all points in between.

"So, where'd ye get aw this crap?" I enquired, again, politely.

"Crap? Yes, I suppose it is now. Some of it used to be valuable, don't you know," says he, finally grasping the English language again. "The world over actually. Many, many places."

"Aye, there's shite everywhere. Ah suppose some cunt's got tae pick it up," I ventured. Charlie was pissing himself.

"Whit's that, then?" I asked.

"Oh, that's scrimshaw, made from a narwhal's tooth. The old sailors used to carve them."

"Fuck's a nearwell?" enquires Charlie, suddenly interested.

"S'wan o' them wee whales wi' the horn stickin' oot," I explained.

"'S'auffy wee," says Charlie.

"It's fae a baby nearwell," says I. Exasperated. But knowledgeable. Not having a fucking clue really. I was just learning to be a cunt back then. Did a good job, don't you think?

Exasperated. I continued.

"They cum oot wi' teeth that size?" asks Charlie, incredulous.

"Shut up, Charlie," I scolded, then turned to our host.

"Ah'm Doc 'n this is Charlie. Whit's your name?" "People call me Moby."

"'N whit people wid that be? Dreamboat?" I said to myself.

Fucking weird, I thought. But given how he looked and acted, you could've called him Rasputin and I'd have went along with it.

"Pleased Ah'm sure. An' whit's this thing?" says I, pointing at another bone.

"That's a bone from the erect penis of an imma-ture donkey's ass," he replied knowledgeably. So the old bastard was alive from the neck up?

I was pretty sure he was taking the piss but didn't pursue it. Oh, I was smart back then.

"N' whit's it used fur, 's got a hole in the end?" "Yes, it's a nose bone. It's where you put the string in to pull it through," says he. Not smiling.

"'S goat drawings on it," I said peering closer. "Fuck me, there's a picture of a dude stickin' it in his nose," I agreed.

I picked the bone up and shivered. Placed it back on its wooden holder and said to myself, Self, I got an inclination, a shiver touching that fucking nose bone. I looked at Moby and he smiled.

"Well, gotta go, Moby. See ye aboot." With that, Charlie and me left.

Walking back to our tent, Charlie says, "Strange dood. Strange name!"

"Aye, Ah agree. Name's kinda like Moby Dick."

"Who's Moby Dick?" says Charlie.

"It's a book. No a dood," says I.

"Ah don't like thay pornographic books," Says Charlie.

"It's no pornographic, 's aboot whales."

"Ah don't like thay Welsh bastards, either," explained Charlie.

I didn't think it was worth it so we just walked home.

∾

I'M SORRY. I WAS SIXTEEN or seventeen at the time and was no connoisseur of anything, let alone art. I remember little pieces of scrimshaw with sailors etchings on them and carvings, lots of carvings, but none remarkable as I recall. In other words, I thought they were junk. A reflection of my life at the time, I'd guess. I was a fucking Philistine from Glasgow and was treated, rightly so, as such.

That's why it was inevitable I got caught stealing. The cops knew it was me doing the thieving but could never catch me at it. I was pulled in several times and quizzed about the milk and shit. I admitted nothing except a stupid little thing I thought nobody would give a shit about.

I admitted to lighting a fire on the beach and baking four potatoes in the fire. That was it. World War 3. I had taken the potatoes from a farmer's field that ran right up to the sand. No fence. I never even had to step over a puny wire fence to steal the spuds.

"Grand Theft Vegey." To misquote a charge in the US.

The next day I was convicted of stealing four potatoes from a field. "It's a fair cop, Doc. Good nab, Nigel. Righteous collar, Colin."

I could just hear those flat-footed bozos praising each other. It's hard being a criminal but even harder when you know the guy who arrested you is an idiot. Of course, I was the other half of this genius equa- tion so, I can't really bitch.

It would have been more difficult stealing treats from a puppy. Or a good idea from a politician. That would be fucking impossible. Maybe you can tell I don't have a whole bunch of respect for our brothers in Congress.

I was sentenced to three months in a detention center. This is almost a prison. Not "Approved

School" not "Borstal." Real honest to God almost jail. Run like a military camp. By the way, not a thing wrong with that.

I was eighteen and furious. Sentence to three months for stealing four potatoes from a field? Was that even a crime?

I stood before three judges who were seated behind a scaffold plank, balanced on three oak beer barrels. In a fucking barn. I shit you not.

There were three guys; one was the butcher, another was the baker. I knew this because one was wearing a baseball cap with the name Fred's Quality Meats on it and the other fucker had on an apron with Dusty Bakers emblazoned on the front.

I did not ask what the other guy did in case the obvious showed up. If the other guy's occupation was a candlestick maker they would've had to scrape me off the fucking floor.

As it was, I needed to be escorted from the room after sentencing, I was laughing so hard and miffed. This was after I miffed one cop in the nuts and another I miffed in the face. Hard.

After an explosion of cops descended on me and joyfully kicked my ass, I decided to give in. Discre- tion is the better part of valor or, as we, from Glasgow can reveal, "Best not get yer ass kicked if truly avoid- able." Wise and contemptuous words leavened over centuries of ass beatings. Thank you.

$$\sim$$

DETENTION WAS LIKE MILITARY CAMP. We were on the south coast of England, very close to the Isle of Wight. Some of the most expensive real estate in Europe. The local environment was a little different.

We were marched everywhere to the sound of spit and polished hob-nailed boots clattering in time to a silent drum in your head. Quite soothing really.

We, the older guys, the ones who had been inside more than a month used to fuck with the screws by marching really well. Ahh! The perversions of the adolescent mind. We thought we were fucking with them by doing exactly what they wanted???

We'll show those fuckers. Let's do this properly. HUH? There were four of us that used to hang out back then.

Everybody was mostly kept inside cleaning and shit except for outside work that needed to be done like picking up trash, moving something to some- where else. Stuff like that.

Getting to walk outside was a holiday and so when those needs arose, the screws would invariably pick us four because, I think, they liked the sound of steel tips clattering on concrete and wooden floors. Especially wooden floors. The screws were all ex- military men and I think they missed the sound.

"I just wanna see a blur," was the favorite phrase of one screw who happened to be an American from Texas. He looked like a grocery clerk and talked like General Patton. He spoke only out of one side of his mouth, so you only saw four teeth. One needed a fill- ing. He had a moon face and glasses and turned out to be not a bad guy in the end. He said goodbye and wished me luck when I was leaving.

We were sent to a detention center as punish- ment, not for punishment, was my opinion then as it is now. I think he felt the same way.

We were meant to be "scared straight" as it were. He would say this "I just wanna see a blur" phrase when we were ordered from "At ease" to "TEN- HUT." That was his word for "attention." He said this with a drawl that John Wayne would have admired.

We were all four outside one time in the gardens growing shit, I suppose, and being guarded by the

American screw, when the siren went off. It only happened once during my stay, so it was pretty rare. We were supposed to form lines for a count to make sure everybody was there.

We dutifully got lined up and counted off. There were only four of us so it wasn't like your "Oxford Treatise test on the price of small coals in China." I don't know if they have a test for your Oxford Trea- tise or not. I just wanted to use the word "Treatise." There I've used it. Satisfied now. "I'm easy pleased" as my mother would say.

After the count we all just stood around wondering what was going on when I blurted out, "Somebody break in, did they?" This somber Amer- ican screw who was always full of business cracked up. Trying to keep his face straight only made it worse. He was howling. I guess all those years of threatening "I just wanna see a blur" had finally caught up.

It took five minutes for him to get a breath and march us back inside. He was still grinning when he handed us off to the next screw.

My time in detention passed quickly. You're kept constantly busy which is a great thing in the slam- mer. There's nothing worse than drumming your fingers and thinking about the life you are missing. That's hard time, buddy.

8

BLACK LIES MATTER

The detention center was near Weymouth off the southern coast of England near the Isle of Wight. I'd ask my buddies in detention where was a good place to visit. It seems I needed to get further away from Glasgow to get straight.

The consensus was the Isle of Jersey.

Jersey is an island nine miles long, five miles wide with fifty miles of sandy beaches. There are no hills. Nothing of consequence geographically. It was as if God had plucked a piece of farmland from Sussex and plonked it ten miles from San Malo off the French coast.

It was rumored to have more bars per square mile than anywhere in Europe. I believe it. At the time there were 600 liquor licensed premises on the island and every year, around March it filled with fresh young adventurous ladies from all over the UK and Europe.

Bugger me gently, did I get lucky. I arrived in Jersey when I was nineteen and left when I was twenty-seven. I used to have a helluva memory. When I was twenty-eight, I could tell you what color socks you were wearing on a specific night ten years prior.

So, while in bed one night, I decided to review my romantic escapades and count how many ladies I had the pleasure of charming over the last eight years in Jersey. Turns out, quite a few. Don't get me wrong, I like and love the ladies, but I seem to have an appetite for lots of them. I've found, in general, they don't like that.

If you read Cosmo and the pages that deal with "relationships" you'll find many hints about the other sex that will amaze you. No clues here. Just let it be said when I was twenty-seven years old, I'd had the pleasure of many women. Not really women. Twenty-three years old, at best, except for one. And not one ugly. Then there was me. Compared to those little girls I was grotesque. I was still trying to find my feet in this new prison-free life when I arrived in Jersey.

Every year there was an influx of stunningly gorgeous young ladies who were out to prove their mommies wrong. That is … all men were not scum and could be trusted. Fuck me, were they in for a rude awakening. All men are not scum? … Some of the ones in cemeteries can be trusted. But only some. Men are men, after all. And these beautiful young creatures were adventurous to boot.

It was the seventies after all, and "the pill" was new and had allowed these ladies license to make love. Beautiful creatures. I thoroughly and enjoyably loved them all. And I was a ROCK STAR, before the term was invented because of my adolescent sopho- moric behavior. TALKING TO YOU, ERICK. Smile!

I knew nobody on the rock (the locals' name for Jersey) when I arrived. I had very little money. Enough for maybe a week in a guest house. So I rented a place for a week, went out that same night to the local disco, met a bunch of great guys who ended up being my friends for the next seven years.

There was Alan Britland, Peter Woods, Peter Morrow, John Connor, Big Tam Hartley, John Smith, Billy Tullet and Eddie Rodden. "Eddie the Rat." Well, what else would his nickname be with a name like Rodden? They were all different and all the same.

A bunch of guys, who unlike my mates in Glas- gow, spent their days trying to avoid fights rather than trying to show how tough you were by getting into them.

Life was good. And easy because nobody had anything. Everybody was in the same boat. Poor, young and horny. Everybody needed a job and the only way to get anything was through somebody you knew. If you were wearing working boots and walked past a construction site they would kidnap you, drag you inside and put you to work.

9

ALAN BRITLAND

Alan, like a few of the other guys, was from Sunderland in the northeast of England. A working-class town close to Newcastle.

They were called Geordies because they supported King George during one of the many wars the English like to indulge in.

In describing a Geordie they used to say, "Think of a Scotsman with his head bashed in." Of course, in Britain, when you generalize about a population it's never very flattering.

Alan was a skinny kid, about six feet tall with a big nose, long hair and kind of hunched over. He was a body man in an auto shop. By all accounts one of the best. He used to fix Rolls Royces and

Mercedes and the like. As I recall, he used to repair those big buses and vans owned by the BBC.

Alan was always the sensible one, who after three years had had enough of Jersey. Enough party-ing, drinking and carousing. You always knew Alan had been out on the razzle the night before because you would catch him rubbing his elbows the next day.

A product of the missionary position he'd say with a grimace.

He decided to go to New Zealand to start a new life.

He was really well liked and had a ton of friends on the rock so when it was time to leave, about twenty-five to thirty guys showed up at the airport to see him off.

The usual banter ensued. "See you next week." "You'll never leave." "You'll be back before winter."

Alan never came back and the last I spoke to him, about three to four years ago, he was still in New Zealand and had just retired. Sounds like he's having a happy life. He just got married again. I hope he lives forever. He was my friend when we were both trying to become men.

What Alan didn't know was, after he left to fly to London and then New Zealand via Honolulu, no less, we all, about twenty-five of us, decided to visit Alderney, another of the Channel Islands.

Alderney was the smallest of the Channel Islands. There were no automobiles on the island. You could walk around the entire island in about an hour but it had two bars and a hotel. We didn't know it then but the "hotel" only had six beds.

We were all half hammered by this time so didn't give a shit. We booked tickets on the fifteen-minute flight that was leaving in about an hour.

When the flight got called, twenty-five drunken Englishmen and Scots showed up at the gate, were ushered onto the tarmac and directed towards what appeared to be a plane under repair. You could see inside to what looked like bench seats the full width of the aircraft.

Little did we know, and if we weren't all drunk would never have complied with it. This was the plane.

"Come on, gentlemen, slide inside," said the captain.

We did, and when we did, he snapped on the sides of the plane like Legos.

Shock was not the right word but by the time the shock wore off, we were in the air for the fifteen- minute ride. We were still finishing our drinks so didn't even notice when we landed.

Twenty-five drunk foreigners stepped off that tiny plane and proceeded to invade the island.

We loaded onto a small bus that drove us to the harbor on a dirt road. The harbor had the only paved road on the island. It ran approximately 1/4 mile up a small incline, past every building on the island. The grocery store, the 6-bed hotel and the bar. There were two other shops, a souvenir shop and a sand- wich shop.

We all piled into the sandwich shop where the owner was stacking shelves behind the counter. He didn't turn around and we were noisy. "What's going on?" we thought. One of the guys decided to try and catch his eye by going behind the counter and waving. That caught his eye.

He turned around, saw this crowd and jumped back, smiled nervously and proceed to fumble with his hearing aid.

Oh no! I thought. Bad move, Sunbeam.

Three or four guys began shouting orders. But not real orders. Incomplete sentences. Intentionally missing letters and words.

6 ha sa chs 5 che pat s n 14 bot mi k. He heard.

We were all drunk so this was fuckin' hilarious. Twenty-five idiots screaming incoherently at the poor shopkeeper who was pounding his hearing aid trying to get it to work. It was working just fine.

These were just inebriated assholes just torturing the guy. Eventually, somebody felt sorry for the guy and told him what was going on. He got pissed and ordered us out.

We were going anyway. "To the bar," said Peter Morrow, loudly. We all turned and made our way fifty yards to the Prince Charlie. One of two bars on the main and only drag.

We charged into the place as quietly as twenty-five drunks could and ordered drinks. It took at least a half hour to get everybody served and settled. We found out that fifty-seven people lived on the rock of which thirty-two were on vacation, two were sick, six were working at the airport and another three were in the stores. Another five were fishing and the rest were in here. Eight guys. In a bar. On an island. In the middle of nowhere. Oh! and the barmaid. Who turned out to be gay. Ha! Didn't take us long to figure out this was going to be a celibate little trip.

There were a few murmurs of resentment. "Who's idea was it to come here?" "Ahh, never mind." "Let's get pissed."

There was a cheer of approval and that's exactly what we did. We drank, bought the locals drinks. They liked that part a lot. Sang songs, laughed and cried and finally staggered outside to the sandy beach and fell asleep until our flight the next morning. When we staggered back in the next day, the same eight guys were still at the bar, all singing the same songs. We had a few more drinks, unwashed, and didn't give a monkey's toss.

We left on the best of terms. Vowing to return, which we all knew would never happen. But a better time was never had by 25 drunken louts in the Channel Islands.

∾

BIG TAM HARTLEY

"They'll never believe it, Tam." "Yeah they will, I'm telling you."

"Bit by an elephant? Not a chance," said I.

We had been working on a small job painting a kitchen. Tam had been painting the uppers and I was working on the lowers. We passed each other and Tam had left the doors on the cabinets open. I stood up too fast, banged my head on the door and split my head open, resulting in a cut that needed five stitches to close. We were sitting in a treatment room in the hospital. Done for the day.

Tam, ever the prankster, decided banging my head on a cabinet door was too tame a story to tell so the idea was to tell everybody I was bit by an elephant.

After all, here I was, all stitched up and bandaged like a civil war soldier. If I had a limp and carried a flute I couldn't have been any more perfect. Jersey was a quiet island. Nothing much happened. So when the hospital got some actual work to do, they went haywire.

A hang nail would've required a visit from a heart surgeon.

An elephant? What else could've possibly done it? We went to the Soleil Levant. The Solly. Our local bar. I wore this huge bandage wrapped around my head.

"Yeah. A fucking elephant. Didn't ye hear about it?" asked Big Tam. "There's a circus just came into town," said Big Tam, talking to the barmaid. "Thought it would be all over town by now."

"Yer arse in parsley," said Laughing Joe Queen. The only man we knew to get thrown out of a bar on four continents, with pictures to prove it.

"Swear to God," said Tam. Next thing we knew, the bar had filled up with everybody at shift change. The chambermaids got off work, the maintenance guys, the front desk people, everybody. And all they were talking about was how Doc had gotten bit by an elephant.

Had to hand it to Tam. He could spin a yarn. The talk of the town that night was me and the phantom elephant.

We had some fun in Jersey. All was forgiven the next day when the town found out they'd been suck- ered. We all had a laugh at the fools who had believed us. Including many of the fools who had!

∾

I GOT MY FIRST JOB with a small contractor who remodeled residential properties all over the island. Construction was booming so getting a job was simple.

I was remodeling a huge house in the country one time, very high-end. A castle really. The owner was Captain Sir Johnathan Sigmund Black. A short man, running to fat with a handlebar moustache joined to his sideburns. We called this job Black Castle. All granite, inside and out. I saw Captain Black but never met him. I did meet his wife.

This woman was six feet tall, intimidating, around forty-five, slim and stunning. She had a bob of dark hair that almost reached her shoulders. Very tall for a woman of this era. Her neckline was smooth, leading to shoulders that fell to her arms and tiny wrists. When you spoke to her, she did not look at you. She couldn't.

I found out later she had an infection that caused her eyes to flutter, and when she spoke, she fluttered while she looked off in the distance, as if she was remembering something important. Sexy as hell.

She had a personality typical of her class. Plummy voice and an attitude that matched. The working class was useful but uncouth and in talking to them you did them a favour by being truthful. A real bitch who had no clue she was being one.

Truth was necessary, even if hurtful, when dealing with Hoi Polloi.

I was mesmerized. I wanted to take her so bad, but hadn't yet worked up the nerve to proposition her. That changed, not because I got more courageous but because she had decided it was time. She would blink and I would drift off. Jesus, talk about a thought about your mom and SEX. Oedipus Rex. Please shoot me.

I remember one afternoon discussing with Frank, the electrician on the job, what he'd been up to over the weekend. He told me he had done nothing over the weekend because he was trying to lose some weight. So, I asked him (trying to be polite, Frank was obese) how much weight he'd lost.

He answered just as Lady Captain Dolly Black was passing. (The title seems a little pompous now.)

Frank proudly answered, "Three pounds, Doc."

Lady Black looked, and shot back, "Frank, darling, if Mount Everest dropped three feet, nobody would notice." That kitty cat had claws.

She could have been gentle with him. Told a white lie, and say, you look great Frank, well done, then rolled her eyes. But that was not how the upper crust dealt with the masses.

I nearly wet myself. They didn't call him "Frank the Cake" for nothing.

It was three days later when Lady Black (that kitty) had an afternoon tea party for several of her friends.

They arrived around two in their chauffeur driven Rolls Royce automobiles, dressed to the nines and speaking as if butter wouldn't melt between their legs. There were five of them. Late thirties, I thought, early forties. Everyone gorgeous, and every one a total bitch.

"Oh, Bunny," crooned Mirabella, one of the bitches. "Just adore your new landscaping. Did you hire that Latin chappie I recommended?" That's actually how they spoke.

"PJ! Oh, PJ! Love that hair color. Almost matches your eyes." PJ had a "wall eye." Total bitch. It would have been nearly impossible for me to have spoken to her without laughing my ass off. She had a tight little body, but I could not have gotten past the eye. The working class had their foibles too. I would have found myself bobbing and spinning like a demented owl trying to catch the right eye. I asked Frank how he knew which eye to go for? He'd been working there a year. He said, "The blue one."

Lady Black greeted them all in the courtyard and escorted them into the dining room on the ground floor. We were remodeling this area so it was draped off with plastic to prevent dust. I looked at them with maddening lust. I despised their phoniness and class but was overwhelmed by my desire for them. If only.… If I knew then what I know now.

I was working in one of the bathrooms close to the tea room. There were two bathrooms back-to-back that had drywall cut out two feet from the floor. I was rewiring something from the basement so was on my back when one of the ladies entered the bath- room. Joanna Westfarther. A complete "See you next Tuesday" C.U.N.T. Whose husband visited Black Castle with his secretary every Wednesday.

Joanna pushed through the plastic, opened the door to the bathroom next to mine, pulled up her wispy summer dress, slid off her frilly panties and proceeded to relieve herself. She had no clue I was there. Too drunk to be aware. But what a pussy. Hairy from her belly button to her ass.

I was on my back looking straight up. My mouth was the Gobi Desert. If I was asked to count to ten, I could not have done it. I decided to take my time rewiring. Every few minutes another lady would enter the toilet to powder puff, adjust panties, and piss. A man of my age had no choice but to peek. If I did not, I would be in danger of being drummed out of the Scottish Club of Under- appreciated Men. Or S.C.U.M. as it was commonly known.

I was twenty-one and each day was an adventure of hard. I could have beat my dick against drywall and dented nothing but the wall.

They had tea (purportedly, it was actually gin) and gossiped for hours. Who was fucking who, who they thought was fucking who, who should have been fucking who. Giggling and drinking.

One distinct little girl, Lady Jemima Gotham Poudre, Jemima to her friends. A cousin of the Queen's nephew, quiet, but when she spoke, she said a lot. She had a TITLE. She was tiny, no tits, pursed lips and a look that said it all. She had been fucked, last year, by a total doofus, a member of the upper crust, so she was still technically a virgin. It was like getting fucked by a hamster in her estimation. These people were ruthless.

She was younger, nineteen years old, and wore a dress with a pink petticoat, much shorter than the others and when she visited the bathroom she made a point of spreading her legs and pulling aside her silk panties to expose her polite cunt.

I was still on my back looking up and quiet. A genteel whiz was my reward. I think she knew. But I never found out.

She was younger and displayed a brazen innocence common to her class. She visited the toilet more often than I thought necessary. A lady should shave more often. Maybe not? She had hair, but not a lot. Only at the mound, nothing beneath.

She was nineteen and loved to ride her stallion, Brutus.

"How's that beast, Brutus?" enquired Lady Caro- line Montgomery. A real bitch, who I thought wasn't getting enough. She lifted one eyebrow. "Is he still as adventurous as he used to be?" She owned the horse prior to Jemima.

Jemima smiled and said nothing, which said everything. Some more vicious little barbs. Then they said their goodbyes.

My workmates were working in another part of the castle so when Lady Black sauntered back in from the courtyard, still waving to her friends, we were the only two in the area. Lady Dolly Black charged into the bathroom.

She burst through the plastic and flung open the door into the room where I was still on my back on the floor.

"Stand up!" she commanded. "I know what you were doing. Jemima was so embarrassed." I knew that was a lie. But one I was willing to accept.

I stood. She glared at me. Fire in her eyes. But more than fire. She slapped me with her right hand and was about to do the same with her left when I caught her wrist.

To understand these people it is necessary to grasp where they came from. They believed they were the over-privileged upper class. They held their posi- tion in society because God had granted them their esteem. They had not earned it. It was bestowed by the Almighty. Therefore unassailable. What followed was their way of returning to nature. It made them become rutting animals again. Porcine playthings of nature. Unlike the elites of today who hold the belief they have earned their position. Well, like Big Tam used to say, "Everybody needs something to believe in."

And "I believe I'll have another beer." They are and were both wrong. That, however, did not stop what happened from being bunches of fun.

I slowly lowered her arm, staring into her eyes. She did not blink. I glared back. She reached out with her right hand, pulled my head forward and kissed me hard on the lips. My head was spinning.

She slipped off her shoes. I reached up beneath her flimsy summer dress, touched the inside of her left thigh. It was wet. She slid her leg over. I touched the inside of her right thigh. She slid that one over too.

We were standing on paper so when I heard the drip falling from between her legs, I kissed her back, harder. Her pussy was sopping. She was wet to her knees. I pulled her panties aside.

She was now at the perfect height for shagging. She bit my shoulder as I slid into her. I had to take her whole weight as I entered. She was tall but at that moment, for me, she weighed nothing.

I came like a racehorse. Hardly had time to enjoy the sensation, when...

"Oh Dolly. Dolly!" Jesus Christ! It was one of the ladies from the tea party.

"Just a mo', Sweetie."

"Oh fuck," Dolly whispered. "Wipe me," she ordered. I pulled off my tee shirt gathered it in a bunch and wiped her pussy, pulled her panties up and smoothed her dress.

She flounced from the bathroom through the draped plastic and hugged her friend.

"Dear me, sweet thing. Are you having work done to your bathrooms? There's quite an odor." Dolly pretended not to hear.

"There it is, my compact. Thought I left it here.

Well, toodle loo. See you tomorrow at the club."

Lady Black did not return to me. She walked off with my sperm inside her. I saw her just as we were leaving for the day. She glanced at me without a hint of recognition. That gorgeous bitch had not changed her clothes. And, I'd be willing to bet, not her knickers either. If this sounds sophomoric, it was. I was. A part of me still is. It does not make it any less true.

$\sim$

MY TIME IN JERSEY WAS like Disneyland populated by horny teenagers. The island was overrun by seasonal workers from the UK and Portugal. The Portuguese, the Pork and Cheesers.

They are the ones who did the real work. All the hospitality drudgery, washing sheets and dishes, cooking and basically keeping the hotel business moving. They showed up every March and April to the sound of "The Stripper." Well, in my head they did.

The other girls, the British girls, were waitresses, chambermaids and receptionists. The guys were mainly construction workers. I painted and hung wallpaper for a living even though I had served two years as an apprentice carpenter.

Carpentry was still my first love but to get set up as a real carpenter, apart from the lack of skill that jail had interrupted, you needed tools.

To paint, all you needed was a scraper, a dust brush and a pair of whites. My partner there was Tam Hartley. Big Tam. A funny, nice guy with a huge honker who was two inches taller than me. I was six feet two inches tall and he outweighed me by twenty pounds. He was the one that had some training in painting.

But I was the one who was a wee bit smarter. I had already figured out you can make more money with a pencil than you ever could with tools. Anyway, Jersey was not for toil. It was for getting hammered every night and fucking. This is borne out by the club that was born in Jersey and I think still exists to this day.

"The Monday Club." This club was not difficult to join. All you had to do was NOT show up for work on a Monday after having been hammered over the weekend. Not exactly climbing Everest or formu- lating E=MC2. Or writing the Kama Sutra. We didn't try to write the Kama Sutra, but we sure did try to emulate the son of a bitch who did.

My buddy Tam was asked once why he only worked four days a week. His reply, "Cause I can't live on three." Tam was a character.

Every night was a shag fest. Before AIDS came along in the early eighties. You could look at that time coming between the Pill and AIDS. Some call it coincidence. I call it divine intervention. Or sheer blind luck.

From work we'd go straight to the boozer, have a few then go back to our tiny apartments, have a shower, get tooled up in our best tackle (I went retro there) and saunter down to the bar.

And there were plenty of bars. I mean tons. Just in St. Helier by itself was the Soly, the Wine bar, on Snow Hill alone there were two bars across the street from each other. A span of maybe twenty-five yards, within that area was another twenty bars surrounded by more within walking distance. And all packed to the gunnels. It was rumored back then, Jersey had the highest number of drinking establishments per capita in the UK. I have no reason to doubt it. Hundreds of bars on an island five miles long by five miles wide. And you could walk everywhere.

When I think of it, no one even owned transportation except maybe a truck for work. You walked everywhere. To do anything. I never heard of anybody on the entire rock getting busted for a DUI in seven years. And everybody was drunk or stoned all the time.

That all changed eventually. Thanks, Candy Lightner. An obnoxious little drunk/druggy if ever there was one, who most likely did the world a good turn and created a whole bunch of enemies in return. Nobody likes a hypocrite, honey. My advice, you ask? Hey, it's my effing book. I can do what I want. My advice is don't scratch your ass with a broken bottle. Don't need to go to the highest cave in Tibet to get that kind of wisdom.

We'd get all geared up, slap on the Paco Rabanne and waft to your choice of disco. There were very few confrontations. Everybody knew what we were there for. Drinking, a little smoking dope, pussy and making enough money to finance these asides. But these were not asides as in a normal, well-led life. These were our goals. It took a lot of anger to brush aside these lofty aspirations. As in, act like a human adult. So we never got angry. We got along, avoided those that didn't comply and generally had a fucking blast. Fucking anything that moved and her pals. Aaoow!!!

The girls never used sex to get what they wanted.

Because sex IS what they wanted.

I lived for eight years in this Paradise.

My first year there I met Angela Stewart. A sweet girl from Newcastle. Way too good for me. She had the kind of personality that lights up a room. The kind of light that shines when there is no light. A truly good person. I used to speak to her a little while I was slipping myself in and out of her pussy.

She was a gem and I did not know it.

Living on this small island, I learned to get along with just about everybody by being on guard 24/7. I knew by then I'd kick the habit of drinking and fighting and being a tough guy all the time.

I learned it was possible to be nice without wondering if they thought you were a pussy.

I learned hard work and hard play were not incompatible and I also learned I was a handsome SOB.

That was my opinion anyway, and I'm definitely sticking to that.

10

MALTA, NOT MY FAULTA, AND NORTH AFRICA

Angie and I went together on my first trip abroad to Malta. It was her first trip to Europe too. By the way, nobody from the UK knew they were European back then. I don't know why. It's just the way it was. Maybe it's different today what with the Common Market an' all. Showing my age there. Nobody talks about the Common Market now.

I should have known things were not going to go well when we left Britain. We got a flight from London to Valletta, the capital of Malta, in the morning and on the flight over, Malta declared inde- pendence from Britain and therefore, the British pound so, in the space of about five hours, we lost 30% of the value of our cash. Not an auspicious start. The landing was bumpy, a prelude to our visit there, I think. A ride on one of those old 4-prop planes tended to be that way.

The place we had rented was okay, if a little spar- tan, but it was on the coast, in a town called Sliema. The local kids were like a lot you'd encounter in semi-third world countries. Brash, arrogant and brazen towards your woman. The kind that performed four-wheel drifts around curves at twenty miles per hour. I was thoroughly unimpressed.

The adults I did like, though. Nice, hardworking religious people. But greedy for money. I suppose the UK had kept them underpaid for years. Hence the breakaway.

Sliema was undergoing massive reconstruction at the time. Building high rises and huge hotels right on the coast. We were there for two days. We took a walk from our rented rooms the first afternoon and watched as bulldozers flatten 2,000-year-old Phoeni- cian arches built into the sea cliffs leading to ancient caves into which longboats used to sail. I was appalled. Angela was not. How could I be such a pig and whine about old arches?

What can I say? I'm a contradiction.

I'm no bleeding-heart tree-hugger but it made me sick to my stomach to watch these ancient struc- tures be demolished by huge yellow bulldozers like that. And Angela's reference to our lovemaking pissed me off. When she got really horny she would call me a pig, then come, violently. I hoped things between us would improve. They didn't.

We left the next day on a plane to Tunis. A forty- five-minute ride to North Africa. Don't ask me why we went there. Because it was close and exotic I suppose.

There's a saying I've used for years that goes, "It always costs you money to learn." How true and I was about to find out why I've used it.

We arrived in Tunisia late in the afternoon. Tunis was a big bustling city. Still is, I believe. Wide tree- lined avenues with impressive facades and minarets. And me, the dipshit that I was, forgot to exchange escudos (The Maltese currency) we had to dinars.

We had about 300 pounds between us. So, the idiot that I was, went to the bank. The bank was impressive. Huge pillars and two massive bronze doors. Trouble was, it was closed. "No problem," said the guards. They got on the phone and called the bank manager who came to our rescue, opened the huge doors and exchanged one of our 100-pound notes for Tunisian money.

What a nice guy. Problem was, while he did not cheat us, he gave us the international currency rate which was about half the real exchange rate. If I'd walked fifty yards up the street, I could have gotten double the money from a street vendor.

We stayed in Tunisia for three days and didn't spend a lot of money so when we left to make our way west across Algeria to Morocco, we still had most of our exchanged 100 pounds left.

We decided to take the train from Tunis, the capital of Tunisia to Rabat, the capital of Morocco and from there make our way to the Canary Islands. We got lucky at the train station and met a young English girl with her Moroccan husband who helped us exchange the almost worthless Tunisian dinars for almost worthless Algerian dinars that he then exchanged for Moroccan dirhams which brought us back to a little over our original 300 pounds.

Talk about luck. We could easily have lost the entire 100 pounds going through government chan- nels. We thanked them mightily, 'cause we all knew we would have been screwed if left to our own devices.

My experience with Arabs has been that they tend to be unforgiving in their dealings with strangers. Not too many scruples, and a belief that money could release you from guilt. So, cheating you for money is almost benevolent. At least they didn't kill you? Right?

Meeting this fresh English rose and her husband who helped us was indeed a godsend. Thank you whoever you are.

The train journey would take three days, so we decided to upgrade our seating arrangements. This cost buttons and we settled in for a long ride. All went well for the first night but when I got up for a piss in the morning, two teenage boys tried to pick my pocket in the corridor on the way to the bathroom.

I smashed one in the mouth, and he ran away along the platform. The other I laid into until the train attendants pulled me off.

I don't speak a word of Arabic, so I tried to explain in pidgin French what happened. Turns out my French was better than the conductors, so he got it. Armed guards came and tried to get me to describe the kids who did this.

They lined up all of the teenage boys on the train. I couldn't pick them out so, I thought, no harm, no foul. We'd just boogie on. But no. While they had them in line, the soldiers went along hitting them with their nightsticks, rifle butts and shoving their heads under water being pumped from one of those old-fashioned cranks you see in old western movies until they found the culprits.

God knows what happened to them after that. I don't really think I want to know. At the time the Algerian government was only mad at the French so being British, we were treated pretty well. Of course, that was fifty years ago so I'm sure things have changed.

I went back to our compartment, kicked out the two other Arabs we were sharing the cabin with, barred the door and pissed out the window for the next two days until we arrived in Rabat.

Pissing out of a train window was no problem for me but it was a little different for Angela. Fortu- nately, the glass slid sideways on this train. Whew! Can't imagine holding her ass up to the windows on British trains. Sure, would've been a sight though.

How my inexcusable behavior would be regarded these days, I'm not sure. But I'm willing to bet it would be different. The authorities were not bad to us. In fact, they did their best to try and help but I was young and scared and being from Glasgow, when you're scared you get violent before your adversaries do.

We got to Rabat at about six in the morning and went straight to the nearest coffee shop for some- thing to eat. We sat down and were immediately accosted by this dude who spoke English with a very posh accent. He was an A-rab but had to have been educated in England at a high-end boarding school.

This was a sleazy little coffee shop next to the train station in an A-rab country. Never the best places in town. After our experiences on the train, Angela was, to say the least, reluctant to deal with this dude but because of his accent and the fact he flashed his passport, I was willing to talk to this dude. It turns out this guy was the Ambassador to Morocco from Algeria or at least in his office according to his passport. He was half in the bag, so I knew he wasn't a practicing Muslim. He wasn't a big guy, and I knew I could take him so when he offered to give us a ride to Casablanca we accepted. Angela was not sure but at this point she trusted me.

Casablanca is about seventy miles from Rabat and we didn't much like the idea of another train journey so we went. The guy drove a little Fiat and when he stopped for gas, he opened the glove compartment. It was stuffed with fifty dirham notes. I mean stuffed. Jammed. Must've been a thousand pounds in there. He bought us breakfast, drove us to Casablanca, booked and PAID a hotel for us, gave us an invite to meet the King of Morocco, Hassan the second, and Archbishop Makarios of Cyprus the next day, then left. I was shocked the next day when he showed up.

The next day he came by, picked us up, drove us to the Palace where we stood in line, shook the King and Archbishop's hands, then drove us back to the hotel, paid for another night and left. Never saw him again. Try making that story up.

Of course, there's always the Yin and the Yang. The next morning, just leaving our hotel, this Arab starts a conversation with us and offers to show us to the local bazaars. When we got to the bazaar, we thanked him and tried to say goodbye. You couldn't get rid of this guy with a fly swatter. He followed us around for hours. We got back to our hotel and tried to ditch him. He then demanded payment for being our guide. I, of course, refused.

No explanation was going to be enough for this dude. So not knowing the strength of this guy, and who his accomplices might be, we decided to leave the hotel. While me and Angela were talking, we thought, "What the fuck, we're going to The Canaries anyway. Let's go now." She agreed.

It was early afternoon, so we drove to the airport and got a plane to Gran Canary Island. As we were pulling away from the hotel we spotted our friend, the guide, with four or five of his buddies making their way to our hotel. Some days you just get lucky.

My hippy days were all like that. Bad days followed by great days. Wouldn't have changed it for the world.

Made it to Casablanca Airport, suffered the usual Arab mistreatment. Angie was stripped of a lot of her clothes before she slapped the little wanker. His (almost) toothless smile would've made a maggot gag. We left Casablanca with relief. North Africa was not for me or Angela. She was a nice wee girl from Northern England, not a wandering fool like me.

I thought it was an adventure. She thought it an inconvenience.

11

TO SUCK OR NOT TO SUCK, WHAT WAS THE QUESTION?

We arrived at Gran Canaria Airport and found our way to the local hippy hang- out. Somebody gave us directions to a camping spot about four hours south on the coast road.

It was full of guys and girls from the US, Germany and Spain. Not many Brits, which surprised me. We spread a sheet out. Didn't need a tent because it never rains there. (really) True enough, during my visit, it never did. We proceeded to get comfortable.

We camped next to an American and his girl-friend. She could do no right according to this guy. And by guy, I mean bitch. This bitch did nothing but bitch. I would have throttled that wanker. Oh!

Don't tell me you did that again! Said the bitch slapping his forehead. I was wishing he was holding a hammer when he slapped himself.

This girl was being henpecked at twenty. "Suck my dick, Julie" "Why'd you do that?" "Suck my dick, honey." "Why'd you do this?"

I was beginning to wonder if this guy even had a dick left given the amount of sucking it was enduring.

We decided to move about five hundred yards to the sand where we sat on full crates of Heineken and got hammered at the local bar. This was during the day. At night we didn't get hammered, we got blootered. The only difference was the length of the hangover.

Hammered was until breakfast, blootered was until after lunch…when the reveries would begin again. Someone had found the wherewithal to buy a new, clean fifty-gallon, plastic, trash bin which got filled every night with bottles of the local hooch and a big block of ice. They called it Sangria. It wasn't. But it did get you moving along the highway to Blooterville which coincidentally had a stop at Hammer Town.

Of course, we always found time for a little dope smoking in between to break the monotony.

My time in the Canaries was not exciting. It was filled with Germans reading Das Kapital, Mein Kampf and The Glass Bead game. What a bunch of fluffing downers those dudes were.

We did go to Maspalomas. I think it means many seagulls. It was a big beach full of middle-aged Germans wearing thongs. Men and women. They say the sand blows over from the Spanish Sahara and forms sand dunes upon which nothing grows unless you're a pervert that likes elderly Teutonic bitches with superiority complexes, in which case your dick might grow. Mine did not.

After I got over trying to be hip and cool, reality struck. We were running out of coin. We stayed on Gran Canaria for about three weeks. The only thing I learned there was the island's name was derived from the old Spanish or Latin name for dog and that Germans, if left to their own devices, become morose and to counter this they either try to conquer the world or listen to Leonard Cohen and his ilk.

We left via ferry to Cadiz the next day and hooked up with an American Jew who possessed the first digital watch I'd ever seen. Very cool at the time. He drove a VW van and had a sign in the back window (also very cool) that said "Gas, Grass or Ass." Multi Christos, was I impressed. Well, I was twenty. This was way before bumper stickers which have enhanced and enlightened our lives with pleasure ever since. (Yeah right.)

Well, I was impressed right up until we got to Perpignan. A little border town in the Pyrenees mountains where he asked us to leave, explaining that our "gas" was used up and since we had no "grass" and I was not willing to share my "ass," we had to part ways.

We did.

Perpignan was a small town on the border between France and Spain. It was populated with Spanish and French citizens who would not cross the road to piss on you if you were on fire. I would call them the scum of the earth if I wanted to insult scum. We had booked into a hotel with no money. Just a promise to pay when our money arrives from our relatives. Which would've been kosher if the French banks did not strike the next day. A dilemma if ever there was one.

We had no money. I don't mean a little. I mean none, nothing, zero. What a fucking leader I was. I was young and was absolutely certain I could scare up some money from somebody back home.

By home I meant Jersey. There was zero chance

of getting any money from my parents or siblings. My parents were always broke and my brothers and sisters were too young. We had been gone for about ten weeks and in ten weeks the economy in Jersey had taken a colossal shit. I knew a lot of people on the island and was sure if I was there, I could've got a job. When I did get back, I found out I was wrong. With a capital ONG.

We had been in the hotel for three days by this time and the owner was becoming a little worried. If worry was indicated by banging on the door at midnight, drunk.

The next day I went to every cafe and commercial petrol station I could find and practically begged any truck drivers I could talk to for a ride. No takers. After five days I finally got a pittance from my buddy in Jersey. Barely enough for one train ticket to St. Malo and the ferry to Jersey.

I did a thing I regret to this day. We talked and I convinced her (Angie) it would be better if I went because I was sure I could round up some cash from somewhere when I got to Jersey.

I got to Jersey three days later and discovered nobody had any money. There were no jobs, and we were royally screwed.

Angie got so scared because of the asshole of an

owner and his ever-increasing advances towards her, so she called her Mum and begged them for cash to get home. Thank God, she sent it. I knew they were fucked too. Her parents were not rich people. They lived in an area of Newcastle called Byker. Poor people refused to move to Byker. Too scuzzy they said.

I was so embarrassed I couldn't look her parents in the eye again. I never did. They never forgave me and I didn't forgive myself either. Right up to this day.

I look back and maybe there was something else I could have tried to get money. I feel guilty as fuck even as I write this. Maybe I thought this would be cathartic, writing this secret I've kept all these years. It's not. I should have stayed there and let her go. Even knowing that wasn't a great idea either. Maybe worse.

Traveling through France was no picnic and then being a stowaway on the ferry was downright dangerous. I had to jump off the ferry at St. Helier and then swim a few yards to shore to get away. No fucking excuse. I'm going to take a couple of days off writing now. I feel like shit.

The only reason I can give was there was nothing I could've done any better. I never made that mistake again.

We broke up after that. No need to wonder why. She still loved me but couldn't trust me. God, I hope her life turned out well. I usually forgive myself on this level. I did not here. No regrets. Right? Fifty years, I still regret it.

12

MARY, MARY NOT CONTRARY

Then there was Mary Carlin. Ahh! Mary. Long straight chestnut hair, about five feet nine inches tall and voluptuous. Yes, that's what you call her. Voluptuous. An ass they would die for today, hourglass figure and talk about tits. I can't because I was attempting to be a gentleman.

It sounds like I'm describing a used car. I don't mean that. She was, and this description does not do her justice, intelligent and fun and beautiful. She was a hairdresser and spoke frightfully posh. Posh for Glasgow anyway. But then anybody who doesn't say "fuck" every other word was posh to me.

Should have married that girl. She would have made an excellent wife. Dispassionately speaking. I liked her a lot but I didn't love her. I wish I knew why. Another one of those "I don't know why" phrases that keep popping up in my life.

When she finally came to the conclusion that we weren't getting back together, she came to visit me and gave me the sweetest goodbye kiss at my front door.

I cried for a half hour because I didn't love her. I should have but didn't.

She left Jersey the next day and I never heard from her or saw her again. We were together for almost a year and I really can't say one funny story or little anecdote about her. That is one girl I feel would've done well for herself. She was smart and beautiful, and I hope she had a shit ton of kids and lived a happy life. God, I hope so.

My only salvation is that we were not together long enough for me to have done much damage.

13

KRISTEN MARIA

Then there was Kristen Maria Hafsteinsdottir. Tall, blonde and leggy, from Iceland. I just loved banging that girl. She was six feet tall, slim and stunning. And she loved to watch TV.

In her home country they would get maybe four or five hours a day of TV time. I found that out when I visited her. So, she'd watch anything. I'd lay her flat on her belly, have her arch her back, stick her ass as high as she could get it, then straighten her arms out in front. She would watch TV and I would get to hump her. I would watch and admire her shape. Just a perfect receptacle for your cock. On my side that was. She, on the other hand, was kind of lazy. She did but not when the TV was on. John Logie Baird has a lot to answer for.

Maybe I, stud that I knew myself to be, wasn't such a stud after all? Couldn't be that! I guess I was still evolving. It was, however, delightful to bang a beautiful woman to the theme of "Howdy Doody." That'll bring you down a peg or two. YOOOOUUU stud muffin!!!!

I was so in love with this girl. Infatuated really. I missed her so much when she left, I borrowed money from my buddy, Peter Morrow, to visit her in Iceland. I arrived in Reykjavik and was introduced to her family. I mean all of them. The whole bunch. Mainly women. She was happy to see me, as were her folks.

Twelve little biddies from the Icelandic countryside. They reminded me nothing so much as Irish fishwives with headscarves and no makeup, very few teeth but kind eyes.

To welcome me they had a dinner party in my honor. I was the special guest and was presented with the best food available, and the highest honor and best seat in the house.

They lived in a condo in a housing estate. Three bedrooms and modern. Very Danish looking with long, low wooden furniture. The living/dining room had a table that could seat fifteen with a stone fire- place on one wall and floor-to-ceiling windows that overlooked a balcony that overlooked the city of Reykjavik. Very high-end home in Iceland in 1973 or anywhere in Europe really at that time.

Icelanders are extremely hospitable people because nobody visited them for hundreds of years. That's unkind. I don't mean to be rude, but they speak a weird language and live in the middle of fucking frozen nowhere.

Their indigenous tongue is, so I'm told, the same as Danish was hundreds of years ago.

You might think a thousand years ago in Britain you would be able to understand the language they spoke in Britain. Still English, right?

Think again, Sunbeam. The Icelanders speak Danish alright but not anywhere near the Danish spoken today. They are not only rural but rural from a thousand years ago. They live in modern European houses and have all the mod cons but in their heads, they think like they are still living in the 10th century.

So, when I say the best food I don't mean steak and scampi. Or pheasant under glass.

I was presented with a full sheep's head, cut off at the neck with the ears still attached and the eyes still in their orbits and looking at you, with little tufts of hair sticking out all over the skull. No wonder that sheep's head had a puzzled look on its face, it was, after all, looking at me.

I thanked them profusely but declined, indicating I couldn't accept such a gracious offer and proceeded to pass it round to the other guests who happened to be my girlfriend's aunts. Twelve of them. Her father and me were the only males there.

The only conversation, in English, was between me, her father and Kristen. There was plenty of conversation going on in Icelandic which would drown out jungle chatter at night. So there was no conversation between me and anybody else. They were not being rude, they just did not know. I felt a little uncomfortable but still welcome, so I decided to break out the whisky. I had brought three bottles of Scotch from Scotland. After that I was everybody's pal. I could have burnt the place to the ground and still been welcome.

The aunts descended on the sheep's head like it was the last chance at life. It's a sight watching a horde of little grannies elbowing each other aside, trying to get the last eyeball at a dinner table.

Her father, Hafstein, was a sweetheart. His name meant "sea stone." Very well educated. A tall hand- some man whose English was nearly flawless.

He was the president of the University of Reykjavik and was married to a woman who barely knew how to apply makeup. Kristen did not think much of her mother but adored her father. In fact, she show- ered with her father until she was eighteen years old. A little odd for my taste. Although as a man I could see the attraction. As a Scot and modern European, I was a little shocked. My granny would have been appalled.

Both she and her father talked about this openly. So there was no shame in their eyes. Me? I found it peculiar, to say the least.

Her father had another habit I found odd. His best friend was a contractor who employed many men doing various construction jobs for the govern- ment. A wealthy man by all accounts. Every Friday night they would get together to play chess. Nothing unusual about that you say. Well, they had a twist that again struck me as unusual.

Her father had constructed a little portable still, wherein he distilled his own hooch.

He had somehow gotten hold of a metal milk urn, inserted an electric heating element in its base with a cooling tube protruding from the bottom, clamped down the lid, threw in some veggies and made alcohol.

How it worked and how it tasted and what kind of alcohol it was, I've no idea, but they would, every Friday night, play chess and drink this rot gut until they fell over. A little strange don't you think? I don't mean the "I'm a little tipsy, I think I'll hit the hay" kind of drunk. They drank until they "collapsed in a heap" type of drunk.

Told you they were a little off. I was there a few weeks and witnessed this every weekend.

Kristen also had a sister. She was like a little replica of Kristen. Her double. She was tall like Kristen and was very smart, like her sister. Beautiful, in an adolescent way and gangly, like a young filly. She was thirteen or fourteen and again still show- ered AND slept with her father on occasion. I don't mean having sex. Just in the same bed.

I really don't think there was anything naughty going on, but these little stories tend to show the gulf that separated the Europeans I knew from what they considered normal. My granny would've had a heart attack. Maybe it says more about me than them.

"I don't make the news, just report it." Supposed to be said in a deep brown voice. Yeah, right.

Kristen and me went out one night, before I got the job, to an Icelandic version of a disco. That was weird. The place looked exactly like a Glasgow version with the round mirrored ball, flashing lights and a DJ that was just as annoying as the Scottish version. The only thing different was, everybody... I mean everybody was hammered. Except me. They sold no alcohol. Was against the law at the time. Icelandic law. The whole country. There were no bars in Iceland. The only place you could buy beer was in the US base at Keflavik. These guys obviously made up for it before getting in.

I got to meet Kristen's ex-boyfriend that night. And his friends. She tried to drag me away before he came over but I was and still am an arrogant bastard. We settled on a handshake and an uncomfortable nod to each other. I found out later his English sucked so he couldn't insult me. He would have looked stupid, trying to goad me into a fight, so he relegated me to a cursory nod and walked away.

But that fucker would have skewered me like a mackerel if his language skills were better. Lesson for all here, boys and girls. Study well at school or you'll never get to punch somebody in the nose.

~

AFTER A COUPLE OF WEEKS, I got a job on a "net boat" and fished in the North Atlantic for two or three weeks after which the captain felt sorry for me and gave me enough for a ticket back to Scotland.

As a fisherman I sucked. I was seasick every day. Spewed all over the fish until all that came out was the dry "boak." Heaves to those who don't speak Glaswegian.

I liked the job on the net boat. I liked the captain and I liked the rest of the crew. Only one thing was wrong. It was on a fucking boat and on boats you get seasick.

There are two things you get to find out about being seasick. The first is, you feel so bad you're afraid you're going to die. The second thing is you're afraid you're NOT going to die.

The guys I worked with were the toughest guys I ever met. I don't think they were special really. Just tough. The way every guy who makes their living from the sea is tough.

The boat was called the Verthandi. (sp) I think it meant aspiration? It was about sixty feet long and maybe thirty-five feet wide with a table running down the middle, waist high. We stood on each side of the table and pulled the net along it, untwisting the fish as they went past. This was aided by a winch that pulled the net up out of the water at the blunt end of the boat.

The captain called both ends of the boat the blunt end and the sharp end except when talking to real fishermen, which I clearly was not.

One day the winch pulled in a shark, dead of course, drowned as all the fish were. Sharks were considered commercially useless. No value to them at that time. So, the first guy on the line picked it up and threw it about twelve feet off the side. This shark was a little over six feet long. I don't know if you've ever tried to pick up a shark six plus feet long but if you have, you'll know it weighs about 250-275 pounds. This motherfucker picked it up with one arm and tossed it twelve feet without a grunt. Nobody on the line blinked an eye. I was impressed.

His name was Thorstein, and he was the nicest guy on the boat. Thank Christ. He'll be dead now. I know this because at that time he was about thirty- five (I was twenty-one) and he drank the local hooch called Brenna Vin (sp). It means burnt wine in Icelandic and tastes as good as it sounds.

He drank this shit all day, every day. That's how I know he's dead. That shit would've killed Andy Capp and he's a fucking cartoon.

Because of my fucked-up condition, spewing all the time, the guys left me alone when it came to doing my shift on watch. I was grateful for this, but it had to end... and end it did, on a night when the swells were, I'm guessing, fifty feet to seventy feet high. No storm, just huge swells.

I had the dog watch that night. Hours between 2 am and 4 am. I knew the swells were massive because I was standing at the wheel watching the radar, making sure we didn't bump into anything…. like fucking land!

My foot was level with my knee, and I was perpendicular. We would rise up the face of the swell, reach the top, the swell would pass, and I'd hear the screw spin catching nothing but air and then SLAM! Down the other side. This went on all night.

I went to my bunk after my shift but never slept a wink. I haven't really been afraid of dying since that night because I'm sure I'm dead now and this is all just a fucking dream.

When we awoke the next morning and looked to the east, there was some land there that wasn't there the night before. Apparently, an undersea volcano had erupted creating an additional land mass. I never saw nor heard a thing but there it was. So much for never slept all night.

That thing could have erupted right beneath us, and nobody would ever have known what happened to us. Dodged a bullet there, Sherlock.

Anyway, my time on the Verthandi, when I and the earth weren't spewing, was great. The guys were extremely polite to one another, very friendly and tolerant of me. I hardly lost any money at cards. Wink wink. Not because I was any good, but I think they kind of admired me for making the attempt at being a fisherman.

At least that's the lie I like to tell myself now. It was, by far, the hardest job I ever tried. I thanked the captain and the crew for their tolerance and got the hell off that boat, vowing never to pull that shit again. I said goodbye to Kristen Maria and her family and headed for the airport. It was Christmas Eve 1973.

One more wee story. When I was leaving at the airport, it wasn't like today when they have huge boards showing every flight and the times, with destinations in English. Everything was in Icelandic, even the announcements. No local dialect followed by English. So, I kind of got lost when my flight was due to leave.

I asked a passing stewardess when my flight was leaving. (All the locals spoke English, even back then.) She looked shocked, grabbed me by the hand, never said a word and dragged me through the doors to the runway.

Ran me full tilt to the jet (a big fucking jet) already taxiing and, still running, waved like a madwoman at the captain in the cockpit who stopped the plane radioed for a stairway to be brought out and got me on board.

Try doing that today. You'd get shot before you hit the concrete. It was Christmas Eve, and I was on my way back to Scotland. Back to my wee granny Findlay's.

I never saw Kristen Maria again. Oh, we spoke a few times on the phone. In fact, I called and left messages, but she knew it was over and so did I. It's sweet in a way because she will always be nineteen years old to me and gorgeous with a tiny crossover on her two front teeth and an infectious laugh. I hope she had a wonderful life.

I learned some things during my trip to this very modern, very backward and beautiful country. I learned I'm not as tough as I thought I was. I'm sure I was a lot less pompous than I used to be. Less of an arrogant prick, I hope.

I learned the Icelandic people are a hardy bunch but kind. They tend to be tall and fit. Probably because they don't drink. They eat stuff I wouldn't flush but that's their choice. Christ, we eat haggis, for goodness sake.

Being on a boat you learn to rely on each other. Even the short time I was there.

I also learned if there's not a God. There should be. Who will you cry to if there isn't? I'd be willing to bet few have sailed the open waters of the North Atlantic who have not asked God for mercy.

Seventy-foot swells will do that to you. So will being seasick for three weeks.

14

FRANCES AND THE MIDDLE EASTERN GENTLEMAN

And almost lastly, Frances Clarke. This one I should have married. I was her fantasy. She would get wet just sitting next to me.

She would wear sexy, anything I told her to, with a total desire to please. Not in a slutty, Las Vegas whore manner, but in a "Your my man and I want to please you," way.

We would be out at one of our local haunts. "Frances," I'd whisper. "Take your panties off."

She'd look askance.

"Ok." Then move as if to get up. "No. Here," I'd say.

"Here? No effin' way," she'd say.

Then I'd whisper something stupid. Like. "I'll give you candy, little girl." Smiling.

A minute later I'd have wet knickers in my hand.

God, she was sexy.

Five feet, four inches tall. Jet black wavy shoulder-length hair. No tits. Didn't care. Nice big nipples and the sweetest, ripest, most fragrant vagina I'd ever encountered. I would slip inside her (she was always wet) and tell her naughty things for hours.

I'd ask her if she ever tried this, tried that. The best thing with Frances was you knew she was hearing these naughty things for the first time, or she was a great actress and enjoying every second of every story.

Either way. You could almost hear her brain tasting the idea, sloshing it around, washing it with her tongue and savoring every last drop. She was beautiful and I was a sewer rat.

We traveled to Greece in 1977. Elvis died that year. Eating a ham sandwich. No, that was Mama Cass. Why do all the good ones die fat? Thinking back, I wish I had died. I treated her so poorly.

Another girl that was too good for me. She was an Irish girl that was brought up as a sweet little

Catholic girl. She had really no interest in traveling like me. I suppose we were doomed from the start.

～

WE FLEW TO ATHENS AND decided to get a room in the Laplaca district. It was a kind of hippy tourist area back then. Close to the Parthenon and a bunch of other historical sites. The whole of Athens is like that, though. Everything's 2,000 years old including the wait staff judging by the time it takes to get served. I'd been there once before, but Frances hadn't so I thought it'd be good for a visit to show her the sights.

We booked into a cheap hotel with a shower and a clean bed but not much else. Went outside and set about looking around. It was getting late so after nosing around the shops for a while, we decided to find somewhere to eat. Greek food sounded good, if obvious. By Greek, I mean where the locals eat. Not "Stavros' Eats" or "Jimmy the Greek's Midnight Cafe."

This part of town really came alive at night when the sun went down. The stores all had garage doors that rolled up so everything was open air. The tables and chairs overflowed into the streets.

Every restau- rant appeared to be one big square room.

Everywhere was busy but we managed to secure a table and watched the world go by for a while. We ordered beer and ate souvlaki and some type of stew. It was delicious. I asked the waiter what kind of meat was used in the stew.

Meaning lamb, pork, beef. You know, a regular question. What gave it such flavor?

He spoke no English. Very few of the regular folk did back then.

He turned to another waiter, mumbled a few words, disagreed for five minutes then, explained, "Meat." Sophocles, he wasn't.

"OK thanks," I smiled. That was 10 minutes of my life I'll never get back.

"I don't like it here," Frances said.

"Why the fuck not?" I enquired pleasantly.

"Look at that filthy Arab," she said pointing to what was indeed, an Arab who was filthy.

"Oh, they're all like that," I explained as if I knew them all.

"Don't like him is all. Looks like a wife beater," she observed. Frances, being a little Irish girl brought up Catholic was told to be nice to everybody. She was. The Irish are the diplomats of the Western World but if they don't like you, look out. She did not like this guy.

The year was 1977, before the world was told we were all the same and equal. Before the world decided Western Society had impoverished the planet and the reason that not everybody bathed every day was because the Western World had used up all the soap. And we were all greedy bastards.

Before we were all tolerant and did not recognize that people like people who like themselves.

"Well, ignore the asshole. You're not obligated to suck his cock."

She made a face, shrugged and went back to watching the world go by. Her face was angelic. Framed by her jet hair. To this day, I don't think I've seen a more beautiful woman. But she could show a little temper at times.

Anyway, the food was good, cheap and filling.

After a couple more beers, we decided to kill it for the night and anyway, I needed to use the john.

As I explained, this restaurant was basically one big room and the toilet was one corner cut off by a makeshift couple of walls.

About six feet by six feet area with eight-inch by one-inch boards slapped on two by four framing. No drywall. You could see between the boards.

They were rough sawn, primitive walls but good enough for at least a little privacy.

Anyway, I got in line behind the aforementioned Middle Eastern Gentleman in the filthy "Djellaba." A kind of floor length, hooded garment common around the Mediterranean.

There was only one toilet/urinal and no toilet paper. I knew there was no toilet paper because there never is. The toilet itself was what we used to call a foot job. Just a slab of porcelain with a place to put your feet and a hole to do your business in.

Anyway, one guy walks out. The Gentleman walks in. Does his business and comes out. I walk in and look down and there was a huge shit, trying, I thought, to climb out of the hole.

I thought, filthy motherfucker never even flushed it. Frances was right. He was a dirty fucker. Now, when I say the john was primitive, I mean it. It had one of those overhead cisterns that has a rope you pull to release the water to get it to flush. So rather than try to piss avoiding the shit, I thought, I'll just flush the thing. Fucking Arab… I muttered to myself as I unzipped Ol' Fagan. My pet name for. Well, you know.

I leaned over, pulled the rope, releasing the water. The water rushed down the pipe, as if glad to be free, hit the turd, which was also delighted, and in turn flew up, covering me in Gentleman shit.

I opened the door to utter silence. You could've heard a mouse fart as I walked through the restaurant. I've heard quiet before but this quiet was deaf- ening. Everyone was extremely interested in what was on their plate. Except Frances. She had her fingers jammed in her mouth. Not making a sound but wetting herself. It was a Friday night, and the place was packed.

Total silence. Until I was about twenty-five yards away. Then the place erupted. Frances was pissing herself. Our friendly waiter was bent over double, howling. For some situations you don't need language. Only a fireman's hose, I thought.

I walked back to the room with Frances trailing. Who wants to walk next to a guy wearing Arab crap?

I was never so glad in my life to get a shower that night. I think it was a year before I could laugh about it. Whenever shit and Arabs are concerned, I'd never dispute Frances again. The next day we did the oblig- atory tours of ancient monuments. They were not as fascinating the second time, but I think that had something to do with the feeling I had about people staring at me and smiling. I'm sure it was my imagi- nation, but I don't know.

Do little kids normally put their hands over their mouths, giggle and point? A few of them seemed to do that to me that day.

I thought I'd better leave before I get a nickname.

I was a wee bit paranoid.

We got cleaned up and left the next day for the islands and the start of our adventure island hopping.

~

WE HAD NO SPECIFIC ITINERARY. Just visit as many islands as possible in the month we had allotted. Our first choice was Mykonos. I had been there three years earlier and had a blast.

It was primitive but friendly. Cheap cafes, cheap rooms but only one hotel. That was fine by me. The beaches were lovely like all Greek islands. The water was like bath water and the waves were great. Pleasant enough to frolic in but not dangerous. We set sail early in the morning. The weather was fabu- lous, so we ended up on deck catching a few rays.

I did notice one thing that was different. There seemed to be a lot more older American people on board than the last time I was here. I shrugged it off thinking it was maybe the month or maybe they had a sale in the States or something.

We sat back and ordered a couple of Mai Tais. That's weird, never had those before. Shit, you were lucky if they had beer.

"How much?" I asked the waiter. Who spoke perfect English. I don't remember the amount, but it caused me to swallow... hard.

Oh well, maybe the ferry has new owners.

"If this is the cost of booze in Greece, I figure we've got enough to last us two days," Frances observed.

"Proly just new owners of the ferry. No competition on a boat you know." We laughed.

We had one other drink on the three-hour ride. Arrived at Mykonos harbor.

"Shit, honey. They've cleaned this place up."

We stepped off the boat onto what was sparkling clean concrete laid out in a random pattern made to simulate slabs of cut river rock. Each piece was outlined in whitewash blazing in the afternoon sun.

Jesus. Looks like God himself scrubbed the place, I said to myself.

We walked to the end of the pier and got on a donkey cart to where my old room used to be. Used to be was appropriate. It was gone and a nice new $100 per night hotel had risen in its place. "Shit honey. This place has changed."

"You paid five pounds a night for this? Helluva deal, hon," she observed.

"I don't think so, honey. The people that stay here would pay more for their dog than I paid for the room. Let's get some beer and something to eat and go sit on the beach and figure out what to do."

"This is not what I remember," I said, feeling a wee bit apprehensive.

We grabbed our bags, went into what can only be described as an exact copy of an American conve-nience store and bought a couple of beers and a couple of sandwiches.

There were Coke and Budweiser signs all over the place.

We went down to the beach, threw out a blanket and lay down.

"It can't all be like this, can't have changed that much. Shit, it's only been three years. There's got to be cheap rooms still around here somewhere. Just got to ask around." We drank our beer and had a sandwich and laid back for a wee siesta, as it were.

"Think I'll take a nap, hon." "Yeah, me too."

I was awakened to the sound of some asshole shouting and somebody else kicking the rolled-up blanket from behind my head.

"What the fuck!"

"Ah. You are awake, sir. In which hotel are you staying?" said this smarmy asshole in a general's uniform. I found out later he was a lieutenant but all these motherfuckers dress like they run the army anyway, so you never know what rank you're speaking to.

"We haven't booked in yet. Just arrived. What's your fucking problem?"

"My fucking problem, as you so eloquently put it, is that we do not allow stinking hippies on our island any longer," he said. In perfect English.

I stared at him. Absolutely dumbstruck. Apart from anything else, Greeks are normally very polite.

They've been the center of civilization for thousands of years and have met people from all over the known world. It's just not in their nature to be rude like this.

"You have two hours to get off our island or I will put you in jail. My men will accompany you until the ferry leaves in one and a half hours. If you do not leave, I'm sure we will be able to find a place for you until the judge can see you in the morning." With that, he turned, said a few words to his men and left.

Well, ol' Jimmy boy might not be the sharpest tool in the shed, but I recognize a GEN- U- INE asshole when I see one.

We packed up our shit and headed back to the harbor, courtesy of the police paddy wagon or what- ever the fuck it's called on Mykonos. I can hardly say the name even now without wanting to spit.

"Well, what the fuck was that?" I said to Frances. "I don't know but I didn't like it," she said. "In fact, I think I'd prefer the company of the fucking A- rab." She turned and looked at me with the begin- ning of a smile on her face.

Thank Christ she was taking it well. I, myself, have taken a lot of shit, but I don't like it when the people around me have to take it. That fucker was one of the most unpleasant bastards I have ever encountered anywhere. I hope I get to meet him in a future life. Preferably as my six-foot four-inch black guy alter ego with the bone through his nose.

We drew a collective sigh, decided to have a very expensive Mai Tai and try to forget all about Mykonos. As I think back, and as further discussions revealed, Mykonos discovered greed. Nowhere else on our trip was like that island.

I've been back to Greece since then and never encountered the same hostility. Neither on this trip nor subsequent trips. Sometimes you just get unlucky.

I think that's what happened to us. Frances and me. I mistreated her by asking her to keep up with me. I should have been kinder. I was quite an experi- enced traveler when we met. I thought we were going on a kind of hippy trip. Bring the bare minimum.

You're not trying to impress anybody so don't bring a lot of superfluous bullshit. I told her this for months. This is traveling, honey. Not vacation. I said to her a hundred times you are carrying what you pack.

I remember to this day what I took. Because mine had been the same for years. A change of shorts, a change of underwear, shaving tackle, change of socks, a sweater and other little pieces of bullshit. And the clothes I had on. Oh, and a waterproof jacket. In a bag you carried by two handles. Not a fucking rucksack.

She took a fucking rucksack and a carry bag bigger than mine. She weighed a hundred ten pounds. I weighed two hundred.

My bag weighed maybe sixteen to eighteen pounds. Hers weighed about forty pounds.

When we left Mykonos, we were still on speaking terms. Every day we were gone from home it got worse. Blazing rows about nothing.

One month later. It was a disaster. She walked behind me everywhere. Always the same distance back. Because I knew where we were going. She was too tired to know.

Of course, I picked up her shit and carried it. But I was so fucking angry, and she was so nonchalant when we left. "Oh, I'll handle it. I'll get it done." I know better. She implied. And determined. And she would not throw anything away. Fucking pissed me off. In fact, she bought souvenirs.

She would not give in and neither of us would admit anything. She could not admit she was wrong and should have listened to me and I would not help her until she admitted she was wrong. Fucking stub- born stupidity. Ahh! The follies of youth. I did help her, of course, but not without extracting the suffering of pain necessary to pay for her wrongness. What a prick I was. I'll say it twice.

What a prick I was. She was worth more than that and I was not willing to pay the price because of my pride. So easy to look back on now and see the errors. I loved her but not enough, apparently.

And there were errors… on me. I was wrong. Badly wrong. I hope she married well (I think she did) (I wasn't that naive) and had some children smarter than me.

15

SANDY AND THE SUGAR DADDY

I was still in Jersey when I met Sandy. I had broken up with Frances but was still in love. What a stubborn dick I was.

Sandy was a good-looking lady. Tall and slim. Only woman I ever married. Well, everybody makes mistakes. The mistake I made was thinking I was smarter than she was.

I could read a book, then six months later if quoted, see the page and the line on the page. I would see the shape of the page. I don't think I had a photographic memory, just a kind of Polaroid that could see indistinct shapes. And hear the echoes of words from the written page.

Sandy could read people. I think she had met the man of her dreams, her first husband ... Tolan. Was it Brian?

Don't recall. Met the guy a few times. He was friends with guys I was friendly with. By all accounts a good guy who had a blast on Jersey, doing what I was doing. He was a very handsome guy. About five feet ten inches tall with long wavy jet black hair. He reminded me of what D'Artagnan should look like from the Three Musketeers.

What we were doing was working, drinking and trying to fuck everything in sight. Until he met Sandy.

He married Sandy. I'm sure he loved her and had a child with her, Louise. Moved to Newcastle, his hometown, went to work one day, got into the back of the work van with five or six of his workmates and was killed in an accident on the way home. I think he was twenty-five.

Anyway, Sandy was wise, I think because of tragedy. She read me like a book anyway. I must have looked like a good substitute to her.

She had minimal skills. No training. A new baby and no man to support her. At least I was a hard worker, so I checked the box for being a provider. She never loved me. Couldn't. She had found her life partner and he was now gone.

Don't know if I truly loved her either. But you need to do your duty. She was my wife, my responsi- bility. So, I ignored my gut feeling telling me this is not going well. It never occurred to me that I was heading for divorce.

We got married in 1978 and were divorced in 1984, I think. I was ordered to pay court costs, about $900 I think and $150.00 or $200.00 per month for my son, Stephen. Nothing for Louise, Sandy and Brian's daughter, which was wrong, and I regret that I didn't even try. Well, she grew to hate me anyway just like her mom. Her mother never forgave me for getting a blow job in Vegas one time at a dart tournament.

If her mother only knew the willpower it took for me not to fuck that girl she might have forgiven me. HAHAHA… NOT. That bitch never let me fuck her for a whole year. Punishment was big for Sandy. Particularly when I was just a meal ticket.

I worked intermittently as a construction worker. Either drywall, painting or carpentry. I was also employed full-time as a salesman for a company that did insurance repair work. I would get the work through insurance companies (through Blackmon Mooring), visit the insured, assess the damage, write an estimate, sell that to the insurance company. Then sell the insured carpet, paint, anything else needed to finish the work then work myself at the weekend to complete the job.

Blackmon Mooring told me they needed a 40% markup. In other words, if I sell a job for $100.00 to the insured and the insurance company, right off the top comes 40% to Blackmon Mooring. The other 60% was to complete the job.

Luckily, I knew what the current costs were and could massage numbers to make everybody happy.

So I thought. When my boss found out I was doing the work, let's just say he wasn't pleased. I was invited to the Queen Mary.

Yes, the real Queen Mary docked lo, these many years in Long Beach California, for a working break- fast with Mr. Blackmon, the National Sales Manager, and my local boss.

The four of us sat round a table in the Queen Mary restaurant. I don't know if they knew why I was there. I sure as fuck didn't. Anyway, it starts civil enough. Usual pleasantries. These were my bosses and my bosses' bosses. I was the only peon invited. Maybe it was the fact that I had brought in $25,000+ the last three months in a row. My end of this was 5% plus a $500.00 car allowance plus my salary (around $35,000 annually).

Mr. Blackmon was droning on about what a great job I was doing and how much he looked forward to working with me in the future.

Then he got to the meat. He explained at length about how great the company was but how it should be better. They had, after all, invented the "Steamatic carpet cleaning machine." They had indeed invented the word "Steamatic" but not the machine. That was invented by "Bissell Homecare."

A short resume of the hierarchy of Blackmon Mooring showed these two guys were carpet cleaners in south Texas who managed to get into a couple of insurance companies' panties and got their work by recommendation who soon discovered it was much more profitable to trash the carpet and sell the insured new flooring than attempt to clean the old one. This led to paint and drywall repair and so on to the point they had expanded their reach to all Southern states.

These two guys got married, Mooring had one son and Blackmon had five sons. All employed by the company. Recently, I saw in the papers that Blackmon was sold to an investment company in New York. This was around 2019, I think.

Back to the breakfast. I was there but not there. I never raised my head from the plate, waiting for the shoe to drop. Mr. Blackmon yammered on about how we were going to increase profits. I wondered how.

Didn't have to wait long. He explained we needed to cut compensation to the salesmen, as well as other assorted shit I didn't care about. He called this an "Austerity Program." He must have read that little catchphrase in a book somewhere because he sure as hell didn't have the wit to invent it himself.

We had been sitting for about an hour and apparently, he was looking for a response from me. Not my boss, not the national sales manager, me. Quick calculation in my head told me that the "Aus- terity Program" would cost me about 50% of my income.

I didn't want to answer so I took a deep breath, calmed down and replied.

"You have effectively eliminated almost 50% of my income. What the fuck do YOU think I think about it?"

My boss didn't say much, he knew me. The other two wankers…. I think one had a stroke and the other seemed to suddenly take great interest in his belt buckle.

I finished my breakfast, assuming the meeting would be over soon. I was right. Five minutes later we were out of there. Five days later I was fired and in fifty years I haven't regretted it for five seconds.

They fell into the same trap every other person and entity has always fallen for involving insurance, GREED. When you dangle this much money in front of a short-sighted, ill-educated greedy bunch of indi- viduals you get corruption.

My boss was a clever little fucker. He was English, short, bald and Jewish. Thinking back, I think he was a CPA. So, he knew every digit intimately. I mean this man knew money. He could make George Wash- ington and Abe Lincoln touch each other in intimate ways that would make Martha Washington blush. I got along well with him. He knew which way was up. The other two bozos sounded like salesmen desperate for a sale. I'm sure they had a degree in "Social Studies" of some description. Probably in "Underwater Basket Weaving" or some such presti-gious degree.

But they had zero street cred. Even an idiot knows you don't cut someone's wages by fifty percent then ask them how they feel about it.

If you cut somebody's wages by ten percent, you're gonna get grumbling, by twenty percent some serious bitching and probably push back. By fifty percent, then you better have three strong men and a squad of nurses at your back to await the coming onslaught.

Apparently, these bozos missed that memo. Which is why they no longer have a presence in Southern California. Within a year they had lost all of their contacts in local insurance companies and a few contracts they had with real estate companies.

16

GOODBYE SANDY

I was around thirty, thirty-two years old and married with two kids. Steven and Louise. I got married to Sandy because I was the boy scout.

Knight in shining armor. The foolishness of a young man feeling bulletproof, thinking he could solve any problem. I was unhappy with my wife and my life. I cheated on her once, if you think a blow job is cheating.

At this time, I was working a lot trying to start a little business. She took care of the house. I took care of everything else. The mortgage at the time was about $450 a month. She got some money because of her late husband's death settlement, so she had put down a bunch of money for a deposit on our house. About 30K. If I remember correctly. Just to clear things up.

I paid for everything for the five or six years we were married and got nothing, zero, zilch when we got divorced. I had paid the mortgage for six years and received no money from the equity she received when the house sold.

Electricity was buttons. So, no worries there. I was also paying for education. $400 each per month for Steven and Louise at Village Christian School. A heavy lift back then for a working man.

Upshot was I didn't like her, and she didn't like me, constant bickering about nothing. Except one thing in particular. I wanted her to get a job.

The kids were picked up for school every day at 7:30 am. Susan then had to "keep the house." Problem for Susan was, a little prior to this she had been hospitalized for ovarian cancer for over two weeks, so I knew what "keeping the house" entailed.

This was in 1984 so her operation was successful. She has lived now for over 36 years past the operation, so I suppose you would say it was successful.

I didn't keep the house. I signed a quit claim deed for no money. I think she walked away with about $50,000.

Meanwhile, while she was in the hospital I went to work and got back in time for the kids' drop-off at 4:00 pm. Weekends were happy enough for me. The kids and I went to parks and the like.

It never occurred to me to ask if they were happy. I just assumed they were. I've been wrong about a lot in my life, maybe I was wrong there too.

I was making Sandy unhappy, though I didn't know why. I've never been the real sensitive type and one day it came to a head.

I came home one day, not in any particular mood. She was sprawled on the floor watching Dallas or Dynasty, one of those mind-numbing shows that allow the body to survive but ensures the brain is steeped and simmering in its own juices.

It was early, five o'clock. No greeting as I walked through the door. Kids were off playing somewhere, just this bitch laying back like some pampered cunt. I walked past her into the bedroom and just shook. I was fucking furious. By this time, I'd had enough. A flash hit me that this was getting no better and would in all likelihood get worse, so I stormed back in to confront her. Bitch hadn't moved an iota. I took a run and with my working boots swung at the TV. Hard as I could. My boot bounced off without a scratch. Of course, this calmed me right down. NOT.

I dove into the bedroom, shut the door and leaned back on it, trying to calm down. There was a thump over my shoulder. About four inches of carving knife was sticking through the door. It was one of those flimsy, hollow core Home Depot doors, another thump and another four inches of blade right where my neck was, appeared. I'd had enough. I wasn't scared. I charged out of the bedroom intending to continue the inevitable fight, telling her you're getting a job like it or not.

Well, turns out she didn't like it. Shock, surprise. Her last words that day and for several months after: "If you make me go to work, I'll leave you." I didn't know if it was a threat or a promise.

I didn't say anything, I just walked to the closet, threw some shit in a suitcase and left. I had left a bad marriage. Have never had any regrets. She was never mine and never would be.

Never spoke to her for six months. Careful what you wish for. You just might get it. It's never good to find out you're the fool and only there for the money. To this day, I can't even look at her.

17

HERE'S MUD IN YOUR EYE

round this time, after going crazy for a while, doing dope and fucking everything with a pussy, I decided to move into an old friend of mine's house in Manhattan Beach. I knew John Smith from the island of Jersey so he knew me when he and I were trying to grow up. I knew he would be kind to me. I needed that then. I was thor- oughly sick of conflict.

He was an old buddy from my dope smoking days on the Channel Islands. He was trained by Willie, a real hippy and a really good carpenter. John became quite the expert carpenter himself.

John was a nice guy, a traveler. Not your vacationer but a real honest to God traveling man who could get to anywhere for nothing with change back. I became a similar kind of dude, though I didn't have the skills John possessed.

I stayed in John's house in Manhattan Beach until he got tired of me. Affluent area.

There was a huge sand hill that Lyle Alzado, an old Raiders player, used to run up on the weekends. He would run by our house on Saturdays with his wife and trainer, so it was a nice neighborhood. Manhattan Beach was a sweet place to live back then. Still is, I'm sure.

I used to hang around a bar called the Chile Bordello. There was always some celebrity there.

Taxi, the TV show was really big back then. Tony Danza came in a few times. Christopher Lloyd too. (Back to the Future) A bunch of famous people at the time. And Raiders. A heap of them.

I met my next victim there. Actually, I think I was the victim but let's not split hairs. Victim is pretty strong here but I was feeling like shit. Nobody likes to fail and I had failed at my marriage.

Her name was Erin Gaffney, and she was a flight attendant for Braniff Airlines. A big girl was Erin. But delicate. Very glamorous, I thought. She was a flight attendant and therefore basically a woman without too many morals. That was my opinion then. Not much has changed.

There's no malice here at all. I loved her. Made her come for the first time ever, and for that, I think she loved me. But only for that. She was too conceited and adored herself too much to really love anybody else. Takes a conceited SOB to know one.

She had a boyfriend in New York that she swore she had left. That was incorrect. (I'm being polite here.) She returned from a flight once and told me she had fucked him. But only once and would never betray me again. Of course.

We had some great times together because of her being all over the world every month. So each reunion was special to a degree. That's why we fucked each other on and off for a couple of years. I was never her type. Not glamorous or rich enough for her. But I did enjoy her. She was bunches of fun.

We were returning from one of our first dates when a most sexually thrilling episode occurred.

I took her to a restaurant in the Valley called Le Petite Chateau. The meal was good, not great but good. As an appetizer of sorts, I ordered a Double Drambuie. I was about halfway through when I noticed something floating in the drink. There was a whole colony of flies in the drink.

I called over the waiter who took one look and pronounced, "Ah, fruit flies."

I told him I really wasn't interested in their pedi- gree and would he just bring the bill. He did and we left, leaving no tip. Pretty shitty thing to do since the service was good up 'til then but I was angry and wanted to impress Erin. A glass full of flies created the wrong impression, I thought.

I was still emotional as we drove back to the beach from the San Fernando Valley. We were almost at the off-ramp to Santa Monica when Erin announced she needed to pee. I say "announced" because it was followed by "Right fucking now."

"Like, right now?" I asked like a dumb ass. Her look was her reply. I turned off the freeway before the Santa Monica off-ramp into a construction site that was just breaking ground.

It had just rained so the soil was muddy. She jumped out of the car took a couple of steps into the mud in her high heels, pulled up her dress, pulled her panties to her knees, grabbed her swollen urethra and began to piss like a racehorse. A golden stream much stronger and wider than I ever imagined.

I was still a little emotional about the fruit fly incident. That only served to raise my pulse. I jumped from the car and before she could finish, I rushed her, threw her on her back in the mud, proceeded to tear off her underwear and got one of the best fucks of my life. I hope she received the same.

I rolled off her, both covered in mud and urine and cum and just lay there sweating and recovering.

We stood up giggling, got in the car and went home to a very long and cleansing shower.

Even the next day I couldn't wipe the grin from my face. I did enjoy Erin but we were destined to go different paths.

What I learned from Erin was a reinforcement of why I was womanizing in the first place. Women are not to be trusted. They will hurt you. So hurt them first. Petty, small-minded and immature but truthful.

I was drinking a lot then which gave rise to Amanda.

18

AMANDA

I had met another girl when Erin and I broke up. She was an interesting girl to be sure. An English girl called Amanda Berrow. I met her in a bar in Santa Monica called the Mucky Duck.

A rocking bar close to the beach and populated by ex-pats, especially on a Sunday afternoon. The place was jumping on Sundays. Great music, jam-packed. Best bar in Santa Monica back then. And that meant the best bar in L.A. And that meant one of the best bars in the U.S.A.

You could walk down a few steps to the sand and if your lady was obliging, screw her on the Santa Monica sand. Amanda was an obliging girl.

Her job in L.A. was a kind of housekeep- er/ babysitter for a neurosurgeon in Beverly Hills but before that, she was the wardrobe mistress for Duran Duran.

Yeah, the real Duran Duran. No joke. She toured with them during their heyday. She knew Simon Le Bon, Nick Rhodes, the Taylors, the whole bunch.

Her brothers owned a nightclub, a couple of bars, I think, in Birmingham, England and they had discovered Duran Duran and kind of nurtured them, by all accounts, to their eventual mega success.

When I met her I didn't know this and didn't find out for several weeks so that had nothing to do with my attraction to her. I liked her because she spoke frightfully, frightfully, had a nice pert figure, seemed very intelligent and last but not least, had a very independent streak.

We palled around for several months and decided to take a trip to Mexico together. She had not seen the Mayan ruins and neither had I. We booked a flight to Mexico City and began a tour of these ancient sites.

It was more of a vacation than I was used to. Nice hotels, public transportation. You know, a vacation, not a journey.

～

WE ARRIVED IN MEXICO CITY by plane and encountered a bumpy landing, which is to say terri- fying. Mexico City sits at about 7,000 feet in the middle of a reclaimed swamp. We just touched down at the exact moment an earthquake hit. The wheels were down, then they weren't. I was thinking who's the idiot flying this thing? We stopped bouncing and reached the gate finally, and everybody stood up to get off. I was livid because having flown hundreds of flights and being a pilot myself, I knew it shouldn't be like that.

We were sitting right at the front and I was going to give that pilot a piece of my mind. I charged up to the cockpit door and knocked angrily. It was opened by a tiny little Asian guy and my first thought, which I regretted later was, "Nobody you can blindfold with dental floss should be allowed to drive, never mind fly a vehicle." When what had happened was explained to me I felt like shit. No I didn't. I just made that up. Just like the Middle Eastern Gentle- man. Trust me, that's a funny story. Let's see if you read it.

She tooled around the area finding all sorts of interesting stuff. I ran up the Pyramid of the Moon. Didn't try to run up the Pyramid of the Sun. Consid- ering my life of debauchery. We had booked a few trips to various vacation spots which were ok consid- ering that's exactly what they were. Nice hotels full of tourists. We also booked a couple of "off the beaten path" trips.

One to a ruin on the Usumacinta River. The biggest river you've never heard of. It actually makes the border between Mexico and Guatemala.

It's about half a mile wide and when we climbed into the dugout canoe about forty or fifty alligators (crocodrillos) on the opposite bank decided to check us out. I don't know if they were alligators or croco-diles. And I didn't want to know. I just knew there was a shitload of them with a shitload of teeth. That should have been made into a shitload of handbags by now.

The ruin was unspectacular but the lunch they served was intriguing. The ride to where the boat was, was a trip in the back of a VW van.

This took eight hours at twelve miles an hour. Speeding if you ask me. The absolute worst road I was ever on. We arrived at where the canoe was.

I don't want to glamorize it by calling it a dock. It was two sticks attached to two planks over the water. The ensuing boat ride was about an hour, and we were starving. The tour of this ruin took about ten minutes and lunch was ready.

Apparently, the "crew" had caught a river turtle and had built a fire onto which they threw the hapless turtle but just before they cooked it in its own juices they proudly displayed it to us for our pleasure.

During this performance, the "crew" member with the biggest bone through his nose made the turtle grimace. I didn't wonder why. I was shocked. I thought the poor animal would have had reptilian teeth because that's what they are. Reptiles.

Not this poor creature, which incidentally, was about twenty inches long and twelve inches wide, had a full set of human teeth. I shit you not. The fucking thing was grinning at me. I knew right then I couldn't eat it. Amanda did. She snaffled it. Juice running from the corner of her mouth.

Like the sheep's head in Iceland, apparently, I can't eat anything that's still looking at me OR grin- ning at me. Told you she was independent.

I didn't want to ask her if she enjoyed it in case she said "Yes."

After all, I still had to kiss the girl. Some things it's best not to know.

After lunch we got back on the boat. Back to the VW. We stayed the night 'cos it was getting dark and fell asleep to the sounds of the jungle. Which if you don't know, is like sleeping next to a fucking jet engine.

In the movies when the star finally gets his co-star into the hammock to the gentle "ooo, ooo" of the monkeys and the "brrr, brrr" of the forest birds, accom- panied by the soothing sounds of the crickets in the background. That's a bunch of crap. It's noisy as hell and very uncomfortable. 'Cause it's hot with insects as big as your fist that'll bite your face off and eat it.

We awoke the next day, dog tired, and headed for our next adventure trip.

This we planned as a trip to an, as yet unfinished, architectural dig.

Remember, we are in the middle of the Chiapas jungle. We got back to almost civilization. Where we did a little tour of the dig we found to be interesting if primitive.

I suppose that's the point. Our hotel was quaint but comfortable, thank Christ. We had a good night's sleep and decided to take a stroll into the mounds of overgrown, as yet to be excavated, ruins.

This was a huge area leading up to what we thought was a path but turned out to be a dry riverbed.

We walked for a good three hours up this path, stopping every now and then to examine these hillocks. We found nothing interesting until we got to the top of the hill where we found we were fucking lost. I'd been noodling along thinking we'd bump into a road soon. Wrong.

We reached the top of the hill, looked over and saw nothing but jungle. Lots and lots of jungle. We had seen no one for hours. No signs, no roads no paths. Nothing. We looked back down the hill we had just walked up and couldn't even see the path we had just taken.

Just then, a local, with a donkey came along.

Thank God. Civilization.

Wrong again. This dude wasn't riding the donkey. The donkey looked like it needed a ride too. It was piled high with corn stalks or some shit and was headed down the hill in the opposite direction we needed to go. I asked him a couple of questions in Spanish; he smiled then left. I don't think this guy spoke Spanish. If he did, he was keeping it a secret.

We were getting tired, and the sun was going down. Amanda was looking decidedly apprehensive.

She wasn't used to this jungle shit and truth be told neither was I. We decided to go back down the hill and hope we'd bump into the path/stream bed we'd followed up here.

I had a feeling we were heading in the right direction and had been walking downhill for maybe fifteen minutes when the Howler monkeys started. Amanda nearly had a fit. She began whimpering and sobbing. I knew what they were. She did not. I must admit when there's a lot of those fuckers, they make a real din. I didn't know how many there were. You can't see the motherfuckers, but it sounded like a lot. Also, I'd only ever seen them in a zoo so I didn't know how aggressive they could be.

So, I started to sing. "I love a lassie a bonny bonny lassie. She's as sweet as the heather in the glen." Don't ask me why. I suppose I thought, "If the Germans in the First World War were scared of us (Scotsmen that is) then maybe the monkeys had heard of us too."

I don't know, but I do know this. We walked maybe another twenty minutes, me singing and annoying everything in earshot until we hit the road to the hotel. Apparently, going downhill is a lot quicker than going up.

I was becoming an old forest dweller. A survival- ist. Amanda was never so glad to see tarmac in her life. She wept with joy and about five minutes later had decided she was going to make this one of her "adventure" stories she would tell her grandchildren.

Amanda was a vacationer, not a traveler. But given she went to a private boarding school for girls, I think she held up well. That was another reason I was attracted to her. Think St. Trinians School for Girls.

It was dark now but we could see the lights of the hotel, so we were fine.

We got back and had food for the first time that day and Amanda went to bed. She was exhausted and I didn't blame her. I had a nap and woke up about two hours later.

The hotel itself while primitive had a restaurant and a bar with real booze. I decided to take a look at the bar. It was a patio bar with huge blue tarps strung between the trees to keep the constant drip off your table. There was no one in the place except for one table with twelve men at it. They were not tourists.

Unless, during my absence, tourists had taken to carrying machine guns over their shoulders. I was still drinking Scotch at the time, so I had a couple of doubles. I was by myself, so I think the barman supplied me with a healthy pour.

After about forty minutes, I was feeling no pain and feeling gregarious. I offered the guys at the other table a drink. Yes, the guys with the guns.

And Scotch no less. Actually, it was really cheap in Mexico even in the middle of the jungle.

The barman went over to them and told them what I'd said. They accepted very graciously.

Mexicans in Mexico are very hospitable people. Unlike the Mexicans I've met in L.A. who, generally speaking, wouldn't piss on you if you were on fire. Sorry, but that's been my experience. They, in turn, invited me to their table so, in order not to insult them, I accepted.

It transpires we were in the state of Oaxaca and the head dude here was the Transportation Minister for the whole state. As I said, there were twelve at the table of which five accepted the drink. The rest of the guys were bodyguards. The dudes with the AKs.

We drank together for a couple of hours. Me speaking broken Spanish and the chief dude speaking better English. We got along well, helped by the Whiskey of course. Not a soul had entered the bar since we got there and I decided it was time for bed.

The chief would not hear of it. I was well-oiled and so was he.

He insisted we go to another bar. Only five miles he said. "OK," I replied. "Let's go." Feeling adven- turous or just maybe hammered.

We went. Thirteen of us in three brand new black Land Rovers. I don't know why I felt no fear. I felt perfectly comfortable driving through the jungle with twelve people I did not know, seven of whom were armed with automatic weapons.

We wound up at a huge wooden gate. Two of the bandoleers jumped out, opened the swing gates and drove up a long driveway, which I couldn't find the next day at gunpoint, if I wanted to. We reached a Hacienda with a massive porch lined with maybe thirty women.

Apparently, the chief's idea of another bar was different from mine. We all sat down, got served appetizers of various kinds and as many drinks as we wanted while two different mariachi bands played.

By this time I was hammered and so when invited to partake of the women, I declined. Only to be told no, take two. Or three, or as many as you want.

I was fucked up but grabbed two so as not to insult. I remember going into the room but nothing after that. I remember the girls laughing and saying something like he only had one of us before they poured me into a Range Rover and drove me back to the hotel.

When I woke up in the morning I found out Amanda knew nothing of my little escapade. That was thirty-one years ago. What a great memory.

A couple of days later we went to visit Puerto Escondido where Amanda lay on the beach naked. She thoroughly enjoyed flaunting herself, that girl. Proud and perky back then.

Well, I think she was only twenty-five. Escondido was a typical tourist spot for Mexico City residents and I'm sure they enjoyed watching this beautiful gringa flaunt herself on the beach.

Then it was back to Mexico City where she caught a flight back to L.A. We kissed goodbye. No regrets. We were friends and it was time to go.

I decided to pull all my money from my bank in the US and continue traveling south until my money ran out. Well, if not ran out, was severely depleted. I had already called the airline and had them change my ticket to a yearly pass. This was back when airlines gave a rat's ass. I was on a path I'd been down before.

The old hippy just left Scotland's path. Wandering the world with no particular destination, no goal. It suited me for the time being. Still pretty screwed up and missing home life. Well, some of it anyway.

19

SAN CHRISTOBAL DE LAS CASAS

W ith Amanda gone with as many of my clothes as I could dump on her, I checked out of the hotel and headed to the bus station. My plan was to head to the Guatemalan border and see what happened.

Not much of a plan, granted, but in my mind, I'd had enough of the US for now. I was doing the same shit, drinking and smoking dope and doing "nose" consistently. Not every day though but that shit needed to stop. Apart from anything else, it was boring.

I got to the bus station and boarded an international bus to the Mexican border town of Tapachula. To explain, there is a world of difference between an international bus and a local. These long-distance carriers are truly world-class, even in 1990. Fully air-con and huge aero plane seats. Very comfortable.

I boarded the bus and headed south. Then... I looked at the map. Exactly opposite of what I'd been doing for years in the US. At last, a travel trip. Not a vacation trip.

The bus ride was maybe twelve hours to what was an old colonial Spanish town complete with a mission. (They all are.) That was not what interested me. I'd seen a hundred of those.

What I wanted to see lay just outside of town.

A local market that happened every weekend and was run by the local Indian tribes.

As we got further south, I was fascinated to see the plant life change. Around Mexico City and its general area, the foliage was mainly scrub and Yucca and cactus. As we got further south, the change was startling.

Wall-to-wall jungle. I couldn't name the plants, but they had huge green leaves and flowers as big as your head. Real jungle. I fell asleep and dreamed of monkeys and sloths and other exotic creatures and woke up at six in the morning in San Cristobal de las Casas.

Just where I wanted to be. I booked into a cheap hotel and got ready for a horse ride. I was gonna do this shit right. My Spanish was getting better. Still not good but improving. I managed to find out where the locals rented horses, found out how much I (a Gringo) should be paying. I was a traveler again.

Feeling pretty good about myself, I got a ride to the stable, rented a horse from two ten-year-olds, who, I found out could ride better than Lester Piggott. I told them I wanted to go to the Indian market and we began to make our way over some serious cliffs. The local kids had a helluva time watching me trying to handle my mount.

That last sentence sounded like I knew what I was doing. I did not. My riding skills were on par with my Spanish. The horses knew their stuff though. Agile little fuckers and strong. They had been over these cliffs many times. I was shocked. They were like goats.

We reached the village and market in about half an hour.

This is what I wanted to see. Row after row of little tents with all kinds of fruits and vegetables. A ton of chicken, pork and some beef. And some stuff I didn't know what it was. That was on the food side of the market. The other side was the Walmart side. Clothes and boots and hats and baskets, just what you'd expect.

What I really came here for was on full display.
A ton of tiny little Indians all in the garb of their
partic- ular village. Each vastly different from the
other. All colors and a variety of hats you couldn't
describe.

When I got off my horse, (notice I didn't say
dismounted.) I was immediately set upon by a
gaggle of tiny, giggling little girls, who I found out
were ten and twelve years old.

I honestly would have said maybe six or seven.
Just tiny, like little dolls. And perhaps the cutest
things I've ever seen. All dressed just like their
respective mamas.

I was there possibly forty-five minutes and they
followed me around the whole time while I dodged
getting poked in the eye by the spokes from the
tent roofs.

The whole market was built for very small
people. I watched the transactions between the
shop- keepers and customers. Much of the sales
were conducted in what I thought was sign
language.

Maybe it was, maybe not, but there was a whole
bunch of laughing and smiling at this gathering.
Not just among my little entourage.

Altogether a very pleasant morning. I'm very
glad I got to see it because I just looked on my

phone (recently) to get the details of distance and the like and was pushed to ads for fucking T-shirts, shots of sparkling fountains, and freshly painted 400-year- old churches.

No village market. No different Indian tribes with their different outfits. No little girls following you around because they've never seen anybody like you.

It made me sick to my stomach. I just zoomed in on my phone. THERE'S A FUCKING WALMART IN TOWN. I just wanted to puke.

I waved goodbye to my little escorts, climbed on my horse and we made our way back to the stable, down the rocky paths to the (Jesus Christ) cliffs and reached the final stretch to the horse paddocks.

Whereupon, those rambunctious little mother-jumpers who ran the stable took off. As did my horse, who thought this was great fun and proceeded at a full gallop to try to buck me off. I swear that horse was laughing at me as I left.

I got back to the hotel. Quick shower. Cold of course. The fuck you think you are? El Pueblo? Pinche cabron. Picked up some swear words as you can see.

Wandered around town for a while. Not many tourists. The ones that were there were mainly

European, doing the mandatory Centro America trip. Ten countries in ten days kind of thing. Very pleasant day. Great fun. Nice meal and after a great night's sleep, got up ready to rock and roll again the next day.

Got back on the bus and headed for Tapachula at the border.

Back then it was a six-hour drive to town. Arrived about two in the afternoon. Booked my usual scuzzy hotel room and went for a stroll around town. Typical border town. (Keep your hand over your wallet and don't fuck any whores.)

I was walking on a side street when I passed this old dude hanging over a half-door, watching the world go by. He was a scruffy motherfucker with wild hair and no teeth. Skinny as a rake, with tattoos of Jesus letting you know he was a good Christian who'd never fuck you. Uh huh! He leans forward and says to me in perfect English.

"Why are you here?" I looked around.

"Me?" says I.

"Yeah, you." Short and sweet.

"Just bumming around," was my reply. "You married?" he enquired. "Divorced."

"What date you get married?" he quizzed.

Who the fuck is this dude? I'm thinking. Okay. No harm.

"September nine, 1979."

"You never stood a chance," he observed, sagely. "Nine, nine 79. Not a fucking chance." And with that, he shut the upper half of the door and went inside. I think he was trying to tell me something, but what that something was, I didn't know then and I don't know now. There it is again. Not knowing shit. The other encounter I had was with a kid in the bus station. I went into the bus depot to enquire about the times to Guatemala City. I was waiting for the brochure when I decided to buy some gum. I bought the gum and caught this kid of maybe five years old looking at me, so I offered him some Chiclets. I smiled and gave the kid a couple.

His hand was still out so I said "bustante." Which I thought meant enough. Which it does. But it's kind of an abrupt, enough. This kid ran off crying to his dad. I felt like shit. Apparently, the correct word is, sufficiente. More polite. His dad got it and smiled at me.

Didn't try to speak Spanish the rest of the day. I had traumatized enough children for that day. Just went shopping and bought nothing. Went back to the hotel. I was glad of the rest. That's the thing about vacations. I always feel I should be doing something. Traveling is a different story. Traveling is the point. Not the reason.

Next morning, I got on the bus to a place called Lake Atitlan in Guatemala. It was a four-hour ride over a mountainous road to a quaint village called San Lucas.

20

GUATEMALA

Guatemala was a lot cheaper than Mexico. I mean noticeably. I hung out in San Lucas for six weeks. Great place. All travelers. No tourists. It was a small seaside town that sat next to a river that hugged the coast like the intercoastal highway. The river, fresh water, ran for twenty miles with nothing but a spit of land between it and the Pacific Ocean.

I stayed in a hut on the spit of land for two weeks and had fun with every single girl in the town. Got drunk every night, staggered down to the river, hopped in a dugout canoe and paddled across to my hut, fell in my hammock and did the same thing the next day. Not a bad life.

You become such a snob when your only restraint is money, not time. I didn't have to be anywhere at a particular time. I had all the time in the world, if I had the money. You start to look down your nose at people who have real lives, like people who have jobs. People who need to get back to school. You know regular folks.

Like my buddy Big Tam used to say, "I've got enough money to last me the rest of my life, providing I die next Tuesday."

∼

LAKE ATITLAN IS A VOLCANIC lake surrounded by mountains and if it was in the US it would have been surrounded by elite condos and million-dollar estates. It's not in the US, so it's surrounded by a couple of poverty-stricken villages. One is mostly an Indian village, the other populated by people of Spanish descent. No prize for guessing the poorest.

I got there on a weeknight so not much was happening. Except the local bars. I think there were four of them. All the same prices. All the same style. I don't know why I liked the place. But I did.

It was dirt cheap at the time which brings to mind a little story.

I was sitting on the beach one very pleasant after- noon. Not your Caribbean white sand beach but a dirty looking, sandy beach, not trashy, just a different colored sand.

It was about eighty degrees and calm, just watching the world go by, looking at the local girls selling T-shirts and shirts made of that local Mayan fabric (probably made in China now) that was so popular when I was there.

The local girls were Indian and wore what they sold. They were short and plump and utterly delight- ful. Always giggling and smiling. Just happy with their lot in life. They couldn't have cared less if you bought something or not. I saw they all had great teeth, these girls.

Must have been the diet because it sure as hell wasn't because of the great dental care available.

While I'm sitting, a sweet little thing walks past, maybe fifteen years old so I start talking to her, asking what she's selling. She's giggling because her Spanish is similar to mine. Practically nonexistent.

I asked her how much for the T-shirts. She quotes more than they are in the US. Okay. I asked how much her Mayan shirts are. She quotes a little less than five dollars. She's wearing some local jewelry, so we have fun pricing the ornaments.

Then, jokingly, I ask how much for her. She never missed a beat.

None of this feigned indignation. No righteous piety. She quotes three dollars in an almost perfect southern California accent.

I know this little girl has never been away from Lake Atitlan. I doubt if she'd even left her village but somebody from L.A. had been fucking this little one.

I must admit I was disappointed. The idea of some surfing bastard or even worse, some bald, fat douche from the San Fernando Valley despoiling this wee girl's innocence bothered me.

I didn't take her up on her offer. She was too young and anyway my sensitivity level had been breached. These people should be left alone in their innocence not subjected to the influences of the western world.

The rest of my stay in Atitlan was uneventful and relaxing. The accommodation was dirt cheap. Spartan but good enough. No point in telling you how much it cost. This is not a travel book. It's about trying to let you know how I ended up the way I did. And it sure isn't a guide. It's kind of like Denny's, the restaurant chain. Nobody ever plans to go to Denny's, you just end up there.

I left Atitlan with some reluctance and headed for the big city. Guatemala City. A dangerous shithole when I was there. I didn't stay long there but I did like Antigua.

Antigua was a town littered with flowers and stucco arches spanning cobblestone streets. It is as clean as anywhere in Guatemala. All of the stores had covered walkways to allow you to window shop in shade, especially around the zocalo, the town square. At night the mariachi band played in the square and the restaurants all opened. Only tourists eat during the heat of the day in the tropics. It was still good to people watch though.

Sitting by a cafe serving drinks that had more fruit in them than liquid. This is the town you visited to learn Spanish. Altogether a very pleasant little place, priced to match.

From there I visited San Pedro Sula. Nice enough town and from there to Puerto Barrios.

I met a local girl there. Forget her name. But she was kind to me and invited me to stay at her place that night. I did not realize she lived with her mom and dad and her three kids.

When I did realize, I decided to buy them two whole cooked chickens. That would save her mom from cooking and have plenty left over. I bought the whole meal dealy. Sides and all.

They lived in a small shack about 10x12 with a canopy over their yard, a table outside and not much else. They all lived in this little hut, three kids, her mom and dad and an elderly relative.

Ate, slept and socialized in this one small space. The Guatemalans are tiny people, much smaller in stature than the Mexicans. Their Indian heritage, I think. But this was even small for them.

She was sweet so I fed them better than they had eaten in weeks and went out to the local disco.

Puerto Barrios is a port city with all that entails. Drunk sailors everywhere who will slit your throat for a centavo and plenty of whores.

An American military ship had just docked that day, so the town was on its best behavior. In other words, cops were standing at two-foot centers. They were everywhere. Too much money to be spent to allow the local thieves to get involved. The politi-cians needed those "Yankee Dollars." I had a few drinks at a shithole bar, then went into the disco. It was full of American sailors and local whores.

I had taken the girl I'd met earlier, and we were dancing when a local thug decided to cut in. I think he knew the girl I was with, and I don't think he was really being impolite.

Anyway, they're playing "La Bamba," probably for the benefit of the Yankee sailors when he decides to cut in. They just reached the line where the words go "Yo no soy marinero." He cuts in. I'm singing, drunk on my ass, at the top of my voice so I sing loudly, "SOY CAPITAN!!"

The kid nearly has a heart attack. "I'M CAPTAIN!!!" I shouted inadvertently in Spanish.

If there's one thing that terrifies a true Latino more than a uniform (even postmen wear epaulettes and have bandoleers of bullets.), it's a title with real power. This dude turned pure white and backed away genuflecting into the crowd.

He thought I was the captain of the American cruiser that had just docked. I tried to explain but he thought I was coming after him. He turned and ran out, knocking people over in his wake.

I thought aahh fuck it and went back to dancing. We left shortly after, and she took me back to her house. I don't think I fucked the girl. I woke up in the morning and had a nice breakfast. Left her a couple of bucks and left. Back to San Pedro Sula where I caught a bus for Tegucigalpa.

I learned a few things during my trip through Centro America. I learned I wasn't gay. I was around forty years old when I did this trip. I wondered why my life was so screwed up. What's wrong with me? Why can't I settle down?

We are all damaged to a certain degree. Still figuring it out. I also learned I'm glad to be living in the US.

Freedom's NOT just another word when you've got nothing left to lose. Try getting dragged off a bus crossing the border between El Salvador and Guatemala for no other reason than you're eighteen and wanted by the army for cannon fodder.

I learned I'm not grateful enough for what I have.

I'll try working on that.

21

JOHN RICKERBY AND MISSED
OPPORTUNITIES

After my trip to Centro America with Amanda had ended, she was long gone by this time.

I returned to L.A. Begged $100 bucks from Erin. I had exactly ten cents. Just enough to call her. I hadn't seen her in almost a year. She told me she wanted to see if she still felt the same about me. She did not. Oh well. She broke my heart once and I wasn't about to let her do it again. I returned to my usual revenge mode. Vengeance is mine, sayeth Jim Docherty against every woman in the world, especially Isabel Murdoch. The one who started me down this road.

I was sitting outside a bar in Manhattan Beach contemplating my journey through Centro

Beach contemplating my journey through Centro

217

America. Feeling a little down. My life was going nowhere and I knew it. The thing I didn't know was if my life needed a purpose. Maybe I didn't have a reason to be. Maybe that was my destiny.

So, I just went about my business working for my friend John Rickerby. They say you go a little crazy when you get divorced. I'll agree to that. Only they said it would be a short journey. Not for me. This was why I think I went to Centro with Amanda. She was not for me and I knew it but looking back, it was a response to getting divorced.

I plowed in with both feet for quite a while. Hitting the booze was my favorite. I liked cocaine, didn't love it but did enjoy the hit.

John ran a small eponymous adjusting company that specialized in overflow work from the govern- ment employee's insurance companies. Mainly prop- erty damage but sometimes "slip and fall" and follow-up to other claims that needed additional info attached.

John was one of those guys you just like. An Irishmen you just gravitated to, always cheerful, quick with a joke and a hearty hello.

He was also the life of the party and could sing like a sparrow. He fucked every one of his friends' wives and everybody loved him.

That, my friend, is a neat trick if you can pull it off. He was a font of knowledge, particularly the current problems in Northern Ireland. (this was around 1984.) He taught me many things, did John, but none more than teaching me to be comfortable around people with power. When John walked into a room everybody knew who was in control. He had a command and usedit.

John passed on several years ago. His wife, Rosie, would not let me see him. She told me he would not know me. He had Alzheimer's disease. Sad. John was a true character. He could give a treatise on iced tea in Israel and make fun of himself the next breath. I miss my friend to this day and will continue to until my breath is gone.

They say you go a little crazy when you get divorced. I'll agree to that. Only they said it would be a short journey. Not for me. I plowed in with both feet for quite a while. Hitting the booze was my favorite. I liked cocaine, didn't love it but did enjoy the hit.

I sat next to Scottie (a younger friend of mine) and watched him stick $800 up his nose in the space of about two hours one night. My metabolism wouldn't let me do that. A half a gram a night was about my limit. Thank God.

I kind of lost my way for a year or two after getting fired from Blackmon Mooring.

I had thought about making at least some of my career at Blackmon Mooring because they had access to real money and power. And they weren't too bright. I had been trained as a carpenter and as an insurance adjuster. They knew how to bullshit, they were salesmen. I knew how to get shit done.

On my own again.

I started doing what I always did when I needed money. I hustled everybody I knew in social situations. Do you need help with anything? Ever done this? Can you do this? Of course, I can.

Somebody finally told me about some dude who needed a two-bedroom apartment painted in a place called Barrington Plaza. A huge five tower apartment complex with about 700 units. I painted the gig, got paid and went immediately to the front office to ask if they had anything else going on.

Did they ever? They were remodeling the entire complex. I immediately threw together a bid. Keep in mind I had about maybe $500 in the bank. The bid included carpet, paint, shelving and was worth about $2.8M for all 700 units. There was profit built in of 25-30%.

I never signed a contract, but they were letting me do a bunch of the work, new wire, shelving, new mirror doors and other petty shit that needed doing. I had done maybe fifty units and the boss seemed happy.

All I had to do was get hooked up with the right carpet guy. Don't want to beat a dead horse so let's just say the douche I finally did get hooked up with owed everybody in town so he couldn't buy credit. I lost whatever chance I had at a nice $2.8M contract.

I never really learned from this debacle because I already knew the lessons. I think they'll become obvious as my story goes on. I messed around like this for a couple of years. Getting close to good money only to see it slip away. I was kind of stagnant at this juncture until God smiled and created two hurricanes in two weeks. Hurricane Andrew in south Florida and Hurricane Iniki in Hawaii.

22

PARADISE LOST

Hurricane Andrew hit first in South Florida. This was a Cat 5 hurricane that blew winds in excess of 165 MPH. It leveled Homestead, a city of about 100,000 people and damaged many more homes and businesses. It cost more than 50 billion dollars and put many companies out of business. This storm essentially sucked up every able-bodied adjuster nationwide so when Hurricane Iniki hit Hawaii, there were no insurance personnel available to handle the claims.

Iniki was a smaller storm but just as intense. It closed down the island of Kauai for weeks but because of the area where it occurred, did not get nearly the publicity Andrew did. Jim Docherty at your service.

I arrived in Honolulu around the 17th, 18th of September courtesy of Custard Insurance Adjusting (CIA) company and was promptly sequestered in the Waikiki Royale Hotel for two weeks. Not a bad gig if you can get it. Everything was paid for. Food, booze, accommodation. This was on Oahu which was merely scuffed by the storm. No real damage. The real catastrophe was on Kauai where just about every building suffered some kind of damage, at least half of which was totaled.

After a couple of weeks, the party was over, and I was shipped to Kauai just in time to see Graham Nash perform in the local school grounds. Great day. The power had been out for a while so the fridges had to be emptied in the big hotels. Perfect excuse for a street party. The entire length of the main drag was commandeered. Probably 600-700 feet long tables jam-packed with lobster, steaks, cala- mari and every other exotic food you could think of. I remember scampi being on the menu. Some of the food lasted for two days and I remember thinking, "Not scampi again."

The next afternoon, desolation. All businesses were closed. All hotels boarded up. You couldn't buy a hamburger. Gas was available but only from the military. Trees were strewn all over the roads.

On top of roofs. If you still had a roof. No phones. This was before cell phones. Power was from generators. What a racket.

There were about twelve to fifteen "adjusters" sent onto the island through our company and we all had to sleep in a two-bedroom condo. They weren't really adjusters. Just roofers trying to get their feet in the door. The condo had six beds. I was lucky. I got a bed. Luck being a relative term here.

The mosquitoes would eat you alive. I remember the first night being kept awake by the constant buzzing of these little bastards. I was exhausted so to try and get some peace, I threw my arm out from under the sheets to let the little bastards feed in the hope the buzzing would stop. It didn't.

It was sweltering hot so I slept with only under- wear on and when I awoke in the morning the sheet that was covering me was splattered in little red dots where the mosquitoes had bit right through the sheet to get at my blood.

Kauai is known as the Garden Isle. A paradise of sorts and today it is. It was no paradise that night nor for several months afterwards.

Eventually the roads were cleared, and the full recognition of the devastation was visible. I traveled the island for a year after the storm and I don't remember seeing one structure that did not suffer some damage. The place was a fucking mess. The Hawaiian people are not built to deal with these kinds of problems.

They have many attributes, but they choose to live in Hawaii for a reason. Because life is laid back and soft. These people are not, on average, your scientists or brain surgeons. They're kind of like the Irish, in a way. They will toil harder than you at occu- pations they like but do not have the work ethic to do work for the work's sake. They will probably outwork you at singing and dancing and playing guitar but introduce a little drudgery into the work and they'll be on the beach like sand, and, like as not, smoking a big fatty. No aspersions here. Just the way they're built.

I lived on Kauai for about five years but visited every island every week when I wasn't working storms on the mainland. I was an adjuster, so I flew at least three to four times a week to various islands inspecting fires, floods, wind damage, you name it. In between I moved to Maui, lived there for about a year and did the same on Oahu. I racked up all kinds of frequent flyer miles so when I flew back and forth to the mainland, I flew first class on Hawaiian Airlines using my upgrades.

By the way, you should never fly first class because it spoils you for the rest of your life. I met

Dog the Bounty Hunter (That could be a good thing in some circles.) in the first-class lounge and sat next to Arlo Guthrie one time in first class. Nice guy. He helped me off with my luggage at Honolulu Airport. I met him returning from a particularly hard storm on the east coast.

I was tired after a hard six weeks solving other people's problems on the Atlantic Coast and was flying back to the Islands for some R&R. I sat in the middle row. Two large leather seats in first class. Two by two-by-two seating arrangements. I tried to read but when the flight attendant came around to take our orders for lunch I had to speak. My accent is quite pronounced and the guy sitting next to me noticed and said, "From Scotland are you?"

"Oh no!" I thought. Another anglophile. I turned to face the guy trying to be polite and saw right away it was Arlo Guthrie.

I smiled and said with all the intelligence of a total dweeb, "Do you know you're famous?" True story. What a fucking idiot. Turns out Arlo is quite fond of his Scottish heritage. He told me he owns a village in Scotland. His dad willed it to him when he died.

Considering I barely owned my own clothes, I was impressed. He was a nice guy. Just going for a job interview on Oahu. Wish I'd get that lucky.

Actually, I was that lucky but his lucky was the "Lifestyles of the Rich and Famous" lucky. Mine was the "Who wants this shit job" lucky. Oh well, I did make good coin in Hawaii. We said our goodbyes and I never bumped into him again. Nice memory for me though.

I lived on the Islands until 1999, made a few friends and many acquaintances. Bob Bentley was one of my friends. He was a contractor on Kauai. The definition of convivial. Just a happy, even jolly guy who was kind to all he met. He knew his shit as a contractor/builder. I know this because I worked for him for a few months when I wasn't adjusting claims on the mainland.

He loved his grandchildren, tolerated his son and couldn't stand his wife. She cheated on him with the milkman. No joke. The fucking milkman. Sometimes when driving with Bob, he would get it in his head to call the milkman and threaten him with grievous bodily harm.

Bob did a great island accent so I'm not sure the milkman knew who was calling him, but Bob would threaten him, his family, his family's graves and everybody he had ever met or heard of. I'd fucking howl into a towel when he was doing this. Bob was a very funny guy.

I had been bumming around the Philippines since 2014 on and off. Bob had visited Cebu in the Visayas in 2019 and decided to stay. He had retired from the construction business on Kauai and had decided to give the Philippines a try. He was fucking around with some prostitute near a shopping mall I used to hang out at, went back to his place where she left her phone on the table while she went to clean up. Bob picks up her phone and comes across my name in her contacts. We had not seen each other since I left Hawaii in 1999. The same whore 20 years later. How's that for a "co-inky-dink."

He called my number and was shocked when I answered the phone.

We talked over the next few weeks about getting a place together in Cebu and arranged to meet just before Christmas 2019.

We last spoke late September 2019. He died October 4, 2019, of a heart problem in a hospital in Cebu. I can't help feeling he'd be alive today if he was in the States. But Bob did like his drink and nose candy, so you never know. He was sixty-eight, I think. We had a great conversation for an hour about all the good times we had in Hawaii. He was in Cebu, and I was in Denver. I miss my friend to this day and feel so sad about the future good times we missed that were barely a couple of months from coming to fruition from the last time we were in contact.

I spoke to his sister a couple of times. She was devastated. He was a well-loved and respected man, Bob Bentley. Never forget you, Bent Shot. My friend.

23

LIVING AND DYING

When I got called for a hailstorm to Denver, Colorado, I knew my time on the Islands was coming to an end so I was kind of looking for a way off the rock. I'd been on Maui for about a year then and didn't like it that much. Oh! great place for a holiday but I was becoming a wee bit sick of Hawaii and the Hawaiians in particular.

Hawaii is the most beautiful place you've ever been. Even the Greek Islands and the Philippines don't hold a candle to Hawaii. But you'll never be really welcome there. Maybe it's the same all over. Like I said, I've never been great at reading people and maybe this is just another example.

So I went to Denver with the intention of scouting it for my next place of residence.

We got the call, Ron Ward and I, around August of 1999 to go to Denver to handle a big hailstorm that hit with three-inch hailstones. Ron was my boss and owner of the company, Global Adjusters.

The hail had beat the shit out of roofs throughout the city, damaging everything from tile roofs to siding and glass and everything in between. I even had a claim from a guy who had just poured his concrete driveway. It was still soft, and the hail beat the shit out of it. Big gouges all over. Kind of unusual to get a claim for concrete from a hailstorm.

When his grandchildren and their dogs saw the mess the hail made they decided to enhance it. Never saw such happy kids and the happiest, filthiest border collie I ever met.

We booked a flight from Honolulu to Denver on a 747, first class, one-way. We didn't care about the cost. (About $700 back then, by the way.) We'd make that and more the first day.

We were both flying first class, but we were not seated together. We had booked late. Ron was in the big cabin, and I was upstairs in the lounge next to the bar. Man, now that's flying!

Ron was pissed. He was my boss and a good guy, but that didn't stop me from rubbing it in. He was the owner of the company and had flown many times in first class, as had I, but never upstairs at the bar. I was sitting facing the bar, behind which stood a blond darlin' from Texas. Y'all. She fed me drinks from Honolulu to Denver practically nonstop.

All that guff about fasten your seat belts and that shit about "When the mask drops." That doesn't happen upstairs in first class on a 747 from Honolulu. I got treated like Zeus the entire flight. A blow job from that L'il Darlin' would have rounded it off nicely but you can't have everything, I guess.

I have recently flown from Manila to New York on United Arab Emirates Airlines on lay flat beds in first class. Very, very nice but it was just not the same thrill I got flying that 747 upstairs at the bar. I'm now officially spoiled for fucking life. I don't care if in the future I'm pampered with an official ball washer, fed bonbons and hydrated with Dom Perignon, it will never equal that first 747 flight.

Anyway, we arrived at Denver International and went to work. We toiled hard for about six weeks and made some serious coin. I think I made about $45K that deployment. Over a grand a day. Was good money back then.

Towards the end of the storm, when things were slowing down, I decided to have a night out. I'd made my money and now it was time to spend a little. I was never a high roller, being quite content with regular guy stuff. Oh don't get me wrong, I loved high-end, expensive shit but only if somebody else was paying for it. Smile.

I went to a couple of local bars in Lakewood and in one I met Stella Riley who would be the boon and the bane of my life for the next five years.

∼

I WAS SEATED AT A crowded bar, the only free seat being next to me. She sat next to me, and we began small talk. She was the assistant manager of the local golf club. Lakewood Country Club. A private club that was once used as a venue on the US Pro Golfers tour. Eventually, it was abandoned by the tour for being too short, but it was still a prestigious club to belong to. All the local businessmen had memberships.

Stella had been married to Jim Riley, a constitutional law professor at Regis University. She had two sons, Scott and Lee, who grew to hate me for reasons you will hear about later. We hit it off that night and though we had to wait forty-five minutes for a taxi, she decided to take me home and fuck my brains out. Which she did indeed. We were both drunk which is why we didn't drive; this enhanced a glorious night of fucking. She really was a spectacular screw. I found out later why.

Her ex-husband was into wife swapping and so was she. This was not an unusual hobby in Denver at this time. In fact, though I was unaware of it at the time, Denver was known as a hub of this particular activity. I don't think this had much to do with Stella leaving Jim Riley, but I don't know. It might have been. I actually think she left him because he was an authoritarian little asshole who was difficult to get along with. But what do I know? Anyway. They were divorced when I met her.

She was a clever girl, Stella, and very obliging sexually. We got along well together mostly, except when she would drink. I took her under my wing and taught her enough to get by as an adjuster for a few years.

In fact, most storms I took her on, she made more than me. A little more, maybe a thousand or two more. But she was always broke. I wasn't.

When we were together, I was making a thousand a day and so was she. Since our finances were separate, I didn't know why this was. I just assumed she was giving money to her kids. I was giving money to Stephen but not a lot. Maybe two or three hundred a month to help with his schooling.

He was going to UC Santa Barbara at the time. I didn't really give a shit about that because I knew he wasn't serious about his education. Or at least he gave me no indication he was.

This sounds like we were rolling in it. A grand a day!! Wow. But that was when we worked and we didn't work a lot, maybe sixty to ninety days a year. That was enough for me but maybe not her. I don't know why, she only made forty thousand at the Country Club. There I go again not knowing stuff, a constant theme in my life.

We were working a storm in Scottsbluff, Nebraska, around 2003 or 2004. I came back to the hotel room after my inspections and found her weeping over her computer. She was crying about money, she said. I gave her a couple of grand. I didn't give a shit about the cash, I had enough. A couple of weeks later when we had finished the job and added up our ill-gotten gains, it turned out she made 1,400 bucks more than me. I had made about $32K, and she had made about $34K. In thirty days.

I don't think it was the money that made her cry. I think it was the drink. I think she saw herself going down a path she couldn't stop and wept for the shame of it.

But like I said, "What the fuck do I know?"

Eventually, she got busted for drunk driving

and other assorted felonies. It started innocuously enough. She left me at the bar one day. It was about five o'clock in the afternoon, to go home.

When I drove home about an hour later, our townhouse was surrounded by cops. She had driven into our complex, blacked out, never turned the steering wheel, and ran straight into our neighbor's unit, destroying her garage and front entrance. Tried to escape by reversing out, hit the accelerator too hard, swerved to try and straighten up and ran smack into our other neighbor's front entrance. Where her car was parked.

She had destroyed two townhouses and two cars in the space of about sixty seconds. That little escapade cost the insurance company in excess of $100,000. And cost her a year in jail.

Her sons and I went to visit every weekend. Well, I went every weekend her sons went when they could.

She got out and went back to helping me with my claims when I could get work. She could no longer work her own claims with State Farm because she called one of their customers a "Greedy Bitch" within earshot of the general manager.

We were deployed to Alabama to work claims on Hurricane Ivan. She died there. Drank herself to death. I didn't even know she was drinking. She became extremely good at hiding the bottles. When they cleaned out our townhouse in Lakewood they found almost 300 bottles of booze, empty, half full and full. Various sizes but damn near 300 of them.

I was devastated. I couldn't see straight for years after she died. My brother Garry was there, thank God. I was a mess and he helped me through it. I cried for days.

I must mention a word about Pilot, the company I was working for. Garry hated them because he thought they treated me badly. They pulled all my files, even the ones that were very close to finished. I didn't feel they treated me badly. Though I felt my life had come really close to the end, I knew, logi- cally, life goes on. Claims need to be settled. Other people have problems, particularly after a huge storm like Hurricane Ivan.

When Pilot Catastrophe heard about her death the entire company came to the complex where I had rented an apartment. I mean fifty or sixty people came and tried to comfort me. Of course, the cops were there too. Where's a cop when you need one? Right? Well, the last thing I needed was a cop then.

They have a job and questioning me was part of that, I suppose. Doesn't make it any easier though. She was fifty-two years old and fifty-two-year-old women were not just supposed to die without warning.

Two years earlier she was warned. We were in St. Anthony's Hospital in Denver. She was in a room where the doctor was visiting us. I say us because she was there because of internal pain she was suffering. I was worried about cancer and heart attacks and strokes. The doctor wasn't.

He knew exactly what was happening. I asked the doc if he wanted to speak to her alone.

He said, "No, I think you need to hear this."

I sat listening to him ask questions of her that maybe I should have asked. A couple of questions stick in my mind. "How much have you been drinking?" and "How long has this been going on?"

I nearly fell off my seat at her reply.

She was drinking two bottles of vodka a day and doing it for years. Shows you how much I was aware. I didn't know she even drank vodka. We were together for three years at that time and I didn't know she drank vodka?

We went out most nights when we weren't working and every night when we were working. Sounds a little odd to be drinking every night when you're working but being we worked out of town, it was normal.

Could be in Atlanta one month and New Iberia

the next and maybe Phoenix after that. It was a nomad's life. One that suited me but obviously not her.

Getting up every day at 5:30, 6:00 o'clock in the morning, working hard in unfamiliar cities dealing with people you don't know, have never met and in all likelihood would never meet again is a tough gig.

Then attempting to reach an agreement about the money they're owed with people who don't know you and have no reason to trust you? That takes some skill, I believe. That's why they paid us a grand a day.

Then, returning to an unfamiliar, sterile hotel room? Not really comparable with a comfy night indoors by the fire. So we, and everybody that does this job, went out after shutting down for the day. Normally around 7:00 at night and tended to try and lose the problems of the day by having a few drinks. Sometimes more than a few. Most times more than a few. No wonder we drink. But for me not to know she drank vodka seemed impossible to me. When she was with me she only drank wine. Of course, I didn't know what was in her bag. Now I do.

The doctor told her in no uncertain terms. "If you continue on this path, you will be dead in two years." Right around two years later here we are. Cardiomy- opathy. That was the diagnosis but not the reason. I believe this was a catchall diagnosis that disguised the real reason. Booze.

She may well have had heart disease, but I think the stress that alcohol put on her system made it worse. She drank herself to death. A cause for which her sons had no problem blaming me. Not their loving father who turned her into a whore by intro- ducing her to his warped sexual perversions. Like enjoying watching other men fuck her. Hi Daddy!!

Hey, we all are perverted to some degree but to get blamed by her sons like that when I was faithful to her and never made her do perverted shit like her straight-laced, bow-tied little hubby did is a reach too far for me. I think she was, like me, always inclined to the possibility of alcoholism but I think that little perv helped, if not pushed her over the edge towards something that would take her life by making her a whore. That's my opinion which, given my excellent record at reading people, is worth not a shit.

Maybe I just miss her. I really did love her, you know.

That was the end of Stella except to memorialize and bury her. Not really bury. Just fire and retire her. She was cremated in Mobile, Alabama, and shipped back to Denver where Jim Riley, I suppose, took care of the arrangements. I couldn't. I was a fucking mess. During our time together Stella was always broke and like I said, I didn't know why. I never did find out but maybe she owed money I didn't know about. I don't know. She had gained two lots of land from her divorce from Jim Riley. One in South Park and one just outside Steamboat Springs, Colorado. She was about to lose them to taxes and other shit I knew nothing about, so I paid whatever was due and she insisted I was put on the deed for this. I didn't care. We were supposed to be together for life anyway, right?

Around this time, I also gave her $10,000 for half the townhouse we lived in. That seemed reasonable to me, and her, at the time after all, I had paid all the bills and mortgage since we met and she had paid buttons to move into the place.

I gave her a check for ten grand and when the time came to sell the place, I couldn't find it.

Jim Riley swooped in and sold it and everything in it while I was out of town and still a fucking emotional mess. A little charmer was our Jim. We had never formalized the transfer of ownership of the townhouse, only the land, so that was the only evidence of the actual transaction I had. I found the check years later after everything was settled so I didn't pursue it. Garry was pissed. He didn't like Jim Riley and looking back, he had good reason.

I was living in a rented apartment somewhere because "Dear Jim Riley" had sold the townhouse Stella and I had owned, and I had to get out. They took everything. Jim and his two lovely sons. Even my clothes. Sold them and the condo. Oh well. That's another story.

As for the two lots of land, I gave them to her sons for twenty grand. They were worth about fifteen thousand for the one in South Park and about fifty or sixty grand for the one in Steamboat Springs at that time. She told me she always wanted them to have something from her and I obliged. The twenty grand for me? I paid off all her debts and called it good.

Her son Lee, a chip off the old block, wondered why I received forty grand from a life policy we had to take out for a loan Stella got. As I said, I paid all the bills anyway. Greedy little bastard. Looking back, I shouldn't have given them shit. They made about $100k from the sale of the condo I paid for anyway. That should have been enough. But a lesson learned. I almost, but didn't, make the same mistake with my next brammer I got hooked up with. The lovely Susan Dier Graf.

24

SUSAN DIER (SHOULD'VE BEEN KILL 'ER)

I met her at a bar somewhere in Denver. I don't remember where and invited her to a friend of mine's party the following Sunday. I knew nothing about her except I wanted to fuck her. That seems to be a theme throughout my life.

I wasn't doing too well. Apart from the many disappointments in my life, I still didn't know the direction I should take. I was a clever guy academically but totally unfocused.

"She looks good to me. I think I'd like to fuck her and give her money." That last part about the money was said internally.

Not good criteria for relationships, I'd venture. Anyway, she was all over me at this party, so I went back to her place, a nice three-bedroom, two-story home with a fully finished basement in Littleton. She didn't have a job. Notice another theme here.

She was divorced with two kids. A daughter who didn't like her (she took her dad's side during the divorce), and a son who was "special." Her son was on dope when I met him, and I assume he still is. He was a nasty piece of work. Overweight and stupid. He outweighed me by twenty pounds and was two inches taller so when he punched me during one of our arguments, it stung. To the tune of about five stitches.

He was a "special needs" child who was spoiled rotten and really needed a man to kick his ass with discipline. I wasn't that guy. I tried to like the prick, but he treated his mother with such contempt, I couldn't. When I met him, he was twelve and the last time I saw him he was nineteen, I think. We got into fisticuffs, and I got five stitches on the lip. He has since deserted his mom and moved to L.A. He couldn't stand her either. I suppose. Smile.

Susan was adopted as a baby along with her sister. Her parents were nice enough folks, John and Lela Dier, from Holdrege, Nebraska. Her father was a lawyer in this small town his whole life and her mother was a housewife. It was his second marriage. His first wife had cheated on him while he was in the service.

I think he was a captain in the army, and I know he had a brother who was a Brigadier General. I know this because I cleaned out his garage which held his locker with his name on it. So, Lela was his second wife, and she couldn't have children. She came from a large family, so I suppose she had the urge to repeat and that's how Sandra and her sister got adopted.

Her mother was a sweetheart, and her father was a lawyer and suspicious of everybody and just to make him more lovable, controlling in the extreme. I think her mother liked me. I know I liked her, but he didn't like me, and he distrusted my motives from the start regarding his daughter. I think he thought I was after his money. Ha! He did own some land though and being the only lawyer in town for his whole life, he had managed to accumulate a stack of property through his benevolence. Yeah, right.

Susan was three months behind on her mortgage when I met her. I caught her up and paid her bills for the next six years. She was able to move into her house because of the prevalent financial climate at the time. If you could fog a mirror, you could get a loan.

She bought this house with no money down, unemployed AND they supplied her with a new washer and dryer as a gift to move in. This type of scrutiny regarding potential buyers is one of the reasons, a few years later, the mortgage crisis occurred and nearly bankrupted the world.

She had no money, and I was living where I didn't want to, so I moved in. She had no job and was kind of cunning, I'd say. A base kind of cleverness. Of course, I didn't think those negative thoughts when we first met. I thought she was funny and smart. She was funny, but a conniving bitch if ever I met one.

After a year of living with me in Littleton she wanted to go back to Holdrege. I was paying all of the bills but her son was still at school so she could not work. I think she resented not having her own money. I know I wasn't too chuffed about it. Keeping a dog and barking yourself, as my mother would say. So, she went back to her hometown and got a job as the Director of the Chamber of Commerce in Holdrege. I think she got it because of her father's connections. I don't know this but it makes sense. No other reason. She never even had a degree.

Anyway, she got fired because, as far as I could tell, nobody liked her. Welcome to the club.

Meanwhile, I still lived in Littleton in her house for which I paid all of the bills as well as throwing her a few bucks to keep body and soul together. I'm sure she was bumming off her dad too and bitching about what a cheap ass I was. She thought she was doing me a favor and I know this because years later, she told me I was lucky she had rented the house to me.

The going rate around then was $1,400…$1,500 per month for her house, never mind all the other bullshit that comes with owning a house. She was a spoiled cunt and didn't know it then and doesn't know it now. Her parents have since died and she inherited a few million, I heard. She'll piss it away, I'm sure.

The mortgage on her house at that time was over $1,800 a month and with electric, water taxes and so forth, I decided to get a roommate to help with expenses. I rented out a bedroom to Todd. AKA Harrison. He hates it when I call him Todd. Smile.

Todd paid me $500 a month plus electricity. I allowed my brother to stay with my niece in the finished basement. Todd was there about two… two and a half years. Until Susan showed up again, then he left or was pushed out. Like me.

My brother Garry was going through some hard times around then. He was trying to get legal in the States, trying to keep some custody of his kid but couldn't get work and was dealing with his own bitch, the lovely, charming and monumentally dumb Mrs. Gina Docherty, at the time so he never paid anything for rent for about a year and a half for the basement. I hope it helped him out a little. He left before her ladyship (Susan) returned. In fact, me and Harrison got into it one time because Harrison thought Garry should be paying a third of the elec- tricity, not just me and him.

That reminds me, I must get that money from Garry. Smile.

During our relationship Susan needed money. Surprise. Surprise. So, she decided she wanted to refinance the house. Problem was, she had no job and no money and coupled with no skills, she was indeed a prize. She had, in other words, "No visible means of support." Except me. I was sure visible. Especially when there were bills to be paid.

I had kept up the payments on the house, so I was ok there. But she needed my help to get a mort- gage. Her father wouldn't co-sign for her, I suppose he'd had enough. I'm sure she bled him dry while she was in Holdrege. She was quite good at manipu- lation. Better than good actually. Spectacular might be a better word. Maybe I'm just an easy mark?

I had a decent job according to my W2s and the mortgage looked good on paper so all she needed was my signature. It wasn't costing me any money, so I agreed. I was on the mortgage a few months before I was getting pushed out. She had stopped fucking me months earlier because she was "going through the change of life." Well, my life sure changed. Wasn't getting no gash. To put it bluntly.

Additionally, I just found out she defaulted on the loan I co-signed for. So, my credit is currently in the toilet. But she'll be ok, her daddy just died and left her a few million. I can't stand my ex-wife but this one takes the cake. I detest her because I did nothing but good for her, she shit on me and now I can't abide her.

So, it wasn't long before I left. It was pretty pain- less for me, given my job was going out of town a lot anyway. I rented a nice apartment in a reasonably good area and managed to secure a spot on State Farm's roster of recommended contractors. That's when we started T.G.F.S.

25

TWO GUYS FROM SCOTLAND

J ust about then my brother and I started a little contracting company called Two Guys from Scotland. We got our work directly from State Farm and we loved it. I don't think there's too much better than being your own boss, liking what you do and making a little coin while you're at it.

My job in our company was to inspect all the damaged properties, write the estimates and deal with the insurance company. I spoke their language so getting them to accept my opinion was easy for me.

The adjusters were overworked, young, enthusi- astic and had a desire to learn from an old hand who'd been around a few claims. I also dealt with payroll and workers comp and other technical bull- shit that held no interest for me but had to be handled.

My real skill was knowing what insurance companies would go for and where they would balk.

Garry's job was to inspect the properties, let me know if I missed something, employ our workers, deal with the homeowners and generally oversee the job from start to finish. He loved his job. Garry likes to be the boss. Smile.

And I loved my job. I didn't mind dealing with adjusters and explaining why we needed more money. I'd been in the business for years and had invented or heard every excuse and reason known to man about why it couldn't be done or if it could be done, why it cost more money.

Unfortunately, I knew at least as much, if not more than our superiors at State Farm. They weren't used to that and didn't like it.

They called us in, a couple of times, I suppose, to get the strength of us. Find out what we were all about and get to know us a little. I think they were used to dealing with contractors and not with contractors who held a degree in insurance. I don't know this, but I think it's probably true that they were a little intimidated. They had been given an

Aye Belong To Glasgow 255

education in insurance and State Farm's idea of what a contractor's education should be.

The insurance education was correct. They were trained well in insurance, but the contractor's educa- tion was the kind you get when you say, "Well, I'm not an auto mechanic, but my father was." In other words, half-assed. I'm aware it's never a good thing to show up your benefactor but I suppose I just couldn't help myself. If somebody's ego is so fragile you need to overlook obvious errors they are making, is that right? That's meant to be a real question. Not rhetori- cal. Well, is it?

Let me tell you. It's fucking A right. You should overlook the errors. I should not have been so smart. Or maybe a better way to put it is not so smart-assed. Garry would not have made that mistake. He's much better than me at faking it. I care if "it" is right. Not if "you" are right. Garry cares about the money. Guess which works best for you in the long run? It was my ego at work as well as theirs.

So, we got fired. That was not a good day but a helluva learning experience. Like a wise man once said, "Experience is what you get when you don't get what you want."

Garry's heard that before. Grin. Anyway, we got shit canned. Not because we did a poor job.

Not because of customer complaints. We got fired because of me and my ego. I knew my shit from both sides and that was our downfall. Years later Garry told me the powers that be at State Farm offered to keep him on if he dumped me. He refused their offer. If I was in his position, I think I would have said yes. But found a way to keep me on. Oh! We would have gotten caught eventually but I think I would have felt better about myself and anyway, it would have been a great excuse to stick it "in the MAN'S eye." That's my comfort story and I'm sticking to it.

There were a couple of halfhearted attempts to get hooked up with another insurance company but nothing real serious. So I swallowed my pride and wrote a letter to EA Renfroe. An adjusting company I had worked for, apologized for almost getting busted for drunk driving and pleaded for my job back. I suppose I whined enough to get them to relent so they hired me back.

I did a few jobs for them. Everything in this busi- ness is temporary anyway, until Columbia, Missouri.

∽

IT WAS A HAILSTORM, AND nothing went right from the start.

I was late for my first nine jobs. Nothing pisses people off more than taking their time for granted.

I arrived at the job site, Columbia, and did what I always do. Did what I've been doing for thirty years. I reconnoitered the area around my hotel to inspect for damage. Just a look to see the damage. To half- assed assess the extent of visible destruction.

I looked at four or five homes, didn't see much and concluded this was a relatively small storm. Reported into the office the next day to pick up my claims and promptly discovered they were twenty-five miles outside of Columbia.

I thought I'd better take a look at the area so I drove twenty-five miles to my first loss.

I spotted the place from the road, drove up a driveway about a quarter mile long and parked beside this mansion of at least a 10,000 square feet footprint. The owners were home so I decided to inspect and take measurements. They were quite glad to see me. I was not glad.

It took me all of six hours to do my work. Normally this would take me half an hour. Driving up to the front of the place did not look bad.

The back of the house was a mess.

I had been assigned thirty claims that morning.

Everyone was the same. Some were worse.

So every appointment that was made took three to four times longer than anticipated. Hence, I was constantly late and got nothing but complaining tele- phone calls to my boss for days right up until the second to last one.

That one I was not only late for but fell off the roof. I slipped coming down the ladder and only fell about maybe seven feet onto a wooden deck. I was taken to the hospital with four broken ribs and an unknown back injury.

I only spent a night in the hospital for observation. No head injury and was released the next day. I stayed in my hotel for another four days attempting to get over the shake up I had given myself.

On the fifth day I drove back to Denver where I got the diagnosis for my back. I had Spinal Stenosis and a compression fracture.

My roof climbing days were over. I continued to get workers comp for months but I knew my adjusting days were done.

I was fifty-eight, fifty-nine years old so I decided to live with my injuries and get some work consulting.

The court, five years later awarded me permanent disability with full pension. This is where I am now, living off my Social Security and my savings.

Luckily, I had almost $200,000 in savings. But that's almost gone now. Well, not quite gone.

I also own my own condo that I bought twenty-three years ago so my mortgage is peanuts and I can, and have, lived off my pension so I'm not worried about running out of cash.

I've spent a lot of my savings traveling and buying vehicles so I can always cut back on that if I need to.

Reading over my words here, I should have many regrets but I don't. I don't see my son as often as I'd like but I think that's a common problem among Oldsters.

My dealings with women were pretty much when I was younger and were mainly caused by me. Not really anything I can do about that now. But about 2015, I was visiting the Philippines and got hooked up with a young lady I've been talking to and visited at least ten to twelve times. She seems nice, God knows I've given her enough time to be mean to me. I think I'll try one of the Philippine islands to finish my days. There's enough of them. 7,000 at last count. Surely I can't fuck up on all 7,000?

26

REGRETS I DON'T HAVE

Who? What? Where? When? Why?

In attempting to round out this wee story, this part of my life, I keep returning to these questions.

I know I got "Who?" Being a narcissist an' all. But I did think I included a whole bunch of others. Many of them funny, all of them interesting. One of my excuses for indulging myself in this book.

"What?" was easy. Description is simple. And usually hilarious. In Scotland, if it's not funny, it's sad. We are not one-dimensional people, it's just that we tend to live at the edges of the spectrum.

"Where?" Again easy. Not complicated to know where you are, physically. Mentally, a different story.

"When?" Do you mean which part of my life? Do you mean at what stage? Do you mean metaphysi- cally? Getting into the weird.

"Why?" Now yer talkin'. That's how come I wrote this book. Trying to figure out why I am the way I am and why I do the things I do. If you figure it out please call me at 1-800-Fuck-You. If I ever meet you, don't make me laugh. You might end up in a book.

ABOUT THE AUTHOR

Jimmy Doc was born and raised in Scotland to working class parents. They were mostly good to him, just rather young and inexperienced in the ways of the world. He was raised mostly in housing estates, called schemes, in Scotland. His particular residence was in one called Castlemilk.

His education was excellent. He had a few great teachers along the way who actually gave a shit and did the best with boring curriculum.

More than anything though, Jimmy Doc's early years instilled in him an insatiable curiosity about everything the world has to offer.

Even the bad stuff, as you can read here.

Printed in the United States
by Baker & Taylor Publisher Services